Why Not Today?

Face Your Fears ...
and Chase Your Dreams!

ERIC DODGE

"Rise above the storm and you will find the sunshine."
–Mario Fernandez

Why Not Today?
Face Your Fears ... and Chase Your Dreams!
by Eric Dodge

First published in 2015
by Eric Dodge Music LLC
www.ericdodge.com

Eric Dodge Music
P.O. Box 910435
St. George, Utah 84791
435-674-4319 · ericdodge@ericdodge.com

ISBN-13: 978-1511909921
ISBN-10: 1511909927

Cover design by Steve Lemmon of Spiral Digital Media
www.spiraldigitalmedia.com

Editing by Shelley Fleming,
Day Labor Proofreading & Editing Services
www.daylaborproofing.com

Additional editing by Laurel Dodge

Also by Eric Dodge: *Baby Steps to Music Industry Success—*
"Making It" as an Independent Music Artist

What others are saying about **Why Not Today? Face Your Fears ... and Chase Your Dreams!** by Eric Dodge . . .

"This book is true inspiration for anyone who dreams big dreams but sometimes lacks the courage to follow through."

—Brad Barton, CSP, Author, Speaker,
World Record T&F Athlete

"Eric has found a way to take his life experiences and teach us all a lesson on how to never give up. Wait until you feel the passion he has for showing others how to face fears and chase dreams.

—Laurie Guest, CSP, Author, Speaker

"Since I have known Eric Dodge he has impressed me with his ability to turn his fears into his passion for helping others. This book is just another example of that."

—Marla Cilley, *New York Times* Best Selling Author
and Mentor to women around the world

DEDICATION

To all of you who struggle with fear, anxiety, depression, and hopelessness. To my loving family, my amazing mom and dad, my grandparents, my friends, and all those who cared enough to be there for me and believed in me from the start. To those whose names I'll never know, and those whose names I'll never forget, thank you. Thank you to my editor Shelley as well as my mother, Laurel Dodge, for spending the hours needed to make this book great. Thank you God, for not giving up on me.

—Eric Dodge

My family . . .

"You gain strength, courage, and confidence by every experience in which you really stop to look fear in the face. You must do the thing which you think you cannot do."

—Eleanor Roosevelt

CONTENTS

FOREWORD

by Jason Hewlett CSP, Entertainer and Speaker

I remember the first time my weight got out of control. I did the ritualistic BEFORE photo, sans shirt, and began the diet. 30 days later all I had lost was 30 days, and my AFTER picture was just as bad as the BEFORE one! I remember wondering if I could ever change my life for the best, or if I was destined to be trapped in the body and life I'd created.

The first time I had a shot at performing on a Las Vegas stage was in the renowned Venetian Hotel. It was a spectacular event! Full house, people there to see little ole me, and during sound check I was at the top of my game. For a certain bit I would leap off the stage, however this time I hadn't quite prepped the landing well enough, and with a spotlight in my eyes misjudged the 10-foot-high stage, assuming it was more like 3 feet. As I fell I realized I was in for it.

Slamming into the concrete floor, my shoes exploded off my feet, suit coat popped off, even my hair became messy somehow. My heels felt as if they were shattered. As the people waited in the lobby I knew it was now or never.

I had a choice to make: I could cancel the show, my shot at a dream, or I could face the fear of limping through my first Las Vegas show on the Strip and just do my best. I took an Advil, said a prayer, and went out there and did all I could do, hobbling around the stage like a 90-year-old in a 23-year-old body.

After that show I was in a wheelchair for almost a week, but the point is: I did the show. Fortunately I have since performed in every major casino in Las Vegas to great success. If you've never heard of me before it's because I'm mostly a corporate Entertainer and Speaker. (I hope you'll enjoy my videos at jasonhewlett.com.)

If you've ever been faced with making up your mind, facing a fear, choosing to do something extraordinary today rather than allowing life's dreams to continually pass you by, then you've come to the right place for a dose of reality from one of my favorite singers and people on the planet.

Eric Dodge, for those who aren't already a fan, is in my opinion one of the great success stories in music, performance, and speaking today. I won't let the cat out of the bag, as he'll give you the details of how he overcame being ruthlessly bullied, moving from school to school as a young man, health and weight challenges, stage fright while on a cruise ship following a national tragedy that forever shaped his destiny, and even fire-walking, but to know his story and hear him sing are both phenomenal adventures.

If you don't have his CDs or haven't listened yet to his music, I recommend you buy them and listen ASAP. I'm talking about turning it up to full blast in your car, windows down, Big Gulp filled, sunflower seeds flying out of your mouth, and try not to smile as he sings. Whether you like country music or not, you will LOVE this music. Don't read this book until you do, because you will be blown away first by the soul, inspiration, and reason behind the songs and how it comes through in Eric's voice.

To then go back and read through this book and find out what got him to the point of having my favorite voice in country music will knock you out. I had no idea the backstory of my friend until reading this book!

All of us have been through hard times, have had dirt kicked in our face after being beaten on a lonesome road, either literally or figuratively, but the question is: What are you going to do about it? Will you get back up and keep on living? Or just lie down and let the vultures devour your existence?

Why Not Today? is the kind of read that will get you to a place of feeling pain right along with the victim of unfairness and violence, and it is excruciatingly relatable. Yet by the end of each chapter, victim becomes HERO once we realize he gets back up, dusts himself off, lives and loves more deeply because of loss, and moves toward his dreams because life is for the living. And you will realize the HERO in yourself.

That is why Eric wrote this book. He believes there is a HERO in all of us, and that TODAY is the day to capture our dreams. We may have allowed naysayers and our own demons to keep us from reaching our potential, but that was yesterday. Like Eric says, why not today?

It's tough to name a favorite chapter but for me it's a toss-up between the vulnerably honest "The Single Life" and the empowering "Break Free." Eric has opened up with such personal, private stories in order to share, to give, and teach each of us, and I'm grateful for it.

I first met Eric as he began making his transition from being solely a singer to implementing a message as a Speaker, and I have been a huge fan ever since. Funny enough, as he writes in a later chapter in this book, he used to be intimidated by me, he says. I find it funny, since I just have to log onto his Facebook page and see that he has about 10x the fans I do, and I look up to him in the same regard. We are peers, and he has MADE IT in a business where most people don't. He's done it the right way, by staying true to himself, blazing his own trail, and is making a difference in the lives of thousands, and eventually millions, of people.

Enjoy this book! Ask yourself how it applies to you. Don't read it and simply say that was great. No, this is a book for taking action, with both the smallest decisions—whether to forgive, to try again, to commit, to face the fear—or to make the big changes that we all talk about making.

The question is: Why Not Today? And maybe, just maybe, I'll let you see my AFTER photo sometime.

—Jason Hewlett, CSP
Entertainer, Speaker, Husband & Father, Author of *Signature Moves: How To Stand Out in a Sit Down World*

INTRODUCTION

Why Not Today?
Face Your Fears ... and Chase Your Dreams

My heart was pounding so hard in my chest that I thought it was about to explode. The palms of my hands were cold and clammy, and the sweat was beginning to run down the back of my neck and forehead. Every salty drop of sweat that would run down from beneath the band of my black cowboy hat would burn my eyes as I would try to wipe it away from my face. Trying to catch my breath was the most important thing in my life right now, and concentration seemed impossible.

There was a ringing in my ears and my chest felt like it was being crushed by the weight of a 5-ton elephant sitting on it. This was a panic attack. But who wouldn't be falling apart? I was about to walk out into a football stadium crowded with over 50,000 people, and sing one of my songs.

There was a giant TV screen and camera crews holding cameras right in my face. How was this possible for someone who so desperately feared being in front of a crowd? Would this be the end? Would this kill me? Even worse, *would I forget the words?*

My mind was so blurred, how could I remember anything? What am I doing here? This was all a huge mistake!

Those were some of the questions that ran through my mind as the announcer loudly said "Please welcome Eric Dodge to the stage," and my band began to play a familiar song of mine. I began to walk down the ramp towards the stage, just as I'd done on so many occasions in the past.

My mind was now on autopilot. Trying to calm down, I began to breathe slowly and deeply.

Everything is going to be OK, Eric. Trust your preparation.

Once the first word of that song came out of my mouth my mind began to free up. Everything became clear—the green field, the audience, the blue sky, my great band—and the show went off without a hitch.

I am not an expert on fear, nor pretending to be an expert on anything. However, my fears at times have gotten the best of me.

Let me be clear about something. This book is not about my journey as a country music entertainer, but it has everything to do with being able to achieve that dream. This book came to life because of my overwhelming desire to help others who struggle with the same issues that many of us have lived with, and still live with today. **You** are the reason this book was written. Let me help you to achieve your dreams. It starts by facing your fears.

We all have fears that control us. It is my belief that if we can control our fears we can accomplish anything. If we master our fears, we master our future. When we are born and when we are little kids we are, for the most part, fearless. Outside circumstances, introduced to us throughout our lives, begin the process of developing fears. When we have a fear of something, we have a reason for it. Something happened to us. Maybe it was something we saw, or a reaction we witnessed from someone we loved. This is where our deepest, most strongly rooted fears come from.

We can push past these fears. Many years ago I started believing that we should face our fears instead of running from them. As part of this hard-won knowledge, I'd like to share some stories from my life that caused me to start living a life of fear. In examining my life, I was able to trace some of my very deep-rooted fears back to these stories.

Many of us struggle every day. For me, there were many sleepless nights. Worry, frustration, doubt, fear, sadness, depression, and anxiety are just some of the emotions I have felt and dealt with at many times of my life. Because of these facts, what you read here is going to be very honest. It will literally make my life an open book.

Yes, it will be very hard for me to write—and hard for me to share. It may be hard for some to read, but I believe it *must* be shared. It is very clear to me that my purpose is to help others, as well as myself, to let go of our fears, let go of what is holding us back, and just let go of what we cannot change.

We have one life to live. Why not see what we can do with it? Why not face our fears! And, **Why Not Today?** Are you ready to begin your journey with me? There is no better time to face our fears and chase our dreams.

Part of the stadium just after I got done performing.
Look at all those people!

1 THE BEGINNING

"The enemy is fear. We think it is hate; but, it is fear."
—Gandhi

Do you remember your childhood? How far back can you remember? Do you remember your house, where you lived, all the details? Many people can't remember much about when they were little, but I remember quite a bit from my childhood.

Looking back, the thing that stands out the most to me was my fearlessness. My imagination was incredible. You would always find me playing superhero or some other fun pretend game, once even running out in front of a car in my Superman underwear, holding up my hand and shouting STOP, literally thinking that car would cease moving. At 3 or 4 years old, wearing my Superman Underoos would surely make me into a real-life superhero.

As a child, I was not scared of anyone. Approaching strangers was never a problem for me, sometimes even embarrassing my parents. Did you start out like this as well? Were you brave and talkative as a child?

A few years later I set up an obstacle course of ropes, trees, cracks in the rocks, and many other things to climb over, to train to be an international spy. I cobbled together a glider—you know, like an airplane—out of my mom's sheets and some metal pipes my dad had stored on the side of our house. Running down a steep hill with this contraption, it really felt as if it would take off and fly! What would happen if I actually did take off? Well, this inventor was just not thinking that far ahead.

At 10 years old a friend and I rafted down a river. We were shoeless, and didn't have any safety gear. Floating happily along in the steady current, suddenly our raft got caught on a tree and popped on us! We both swam frantically towards the shore, pulling our deflated raft. Of course, nobody even knew where we were. Getting home barefoot proved to be quite an adventure as well, and we had sore feet for weeks.

Our playground included caves we would crawl into, tunnels for the underground forts we would dig, and tree houses we'd swing from on ropes. Out of all these things we did, never did we think we could get hurt.

The climbing, running, digging, building, and swinging was down to an art. Then after watching Indiana Jones, I decided that I wanted to be an archaeologist—really wanting to live a life of adventure, just like Indy did. Nothing back then scared me at all, and no accomplishment was out of reach.

What was doubt? Not knowing what doubt was back then, it simply wasn't an option—and neither was failure. All that was needed was to decide what I wanted to be when I grew up, and there would be nothing stopping me from being that.

Then slowly but surely, my dreams began to fade. Fear and doubt crept up, and somehow began to change who I was! Over the course of a few short years I went from believing I could do and be anything, to becoming very depressed, closed off, angry, overweight, and defeated. But what made these changes? What could have set my life and my future on a course that was never intended? Something caused me to go from seeking a life of adventure to becoming a hopelessly depressed, overweight adult, a college drop-out, and going from Captain Fearless to a guy who was ready to call it quits. How could I get back that innocence and magic, and reclaim my life full of hopes and dreams? What went wrong?

Well, the answers to these questions emerged from studying my own life. Studying different situations that stood out in my mind, it seemed that every fear I had developed came from a circumstance or experience in my life. All of my fears were in fact built to protect me, and to keep me from getting hurt again. We all have this response, and we all go through this. Realizing this truth, I am going to share with you many stories from my life that are difficult for me to tell. But these stories are very important, because you also have stories that have happened to you. We all do.

Many of you may be holding onto remnants of your stories. As you hold on, these remnants may be holding you back from living the life of your dreams. My hope is that by sharing with you what I have gone through on the path of discovering my purpose, that you can also break free from those things in your past that keep you from moving ahead. For as soon as I faced my past and faced my demons, I began to take small steps to beating my fears.

My life is so much better now. It hasn't been easy and it has not happened overnight, but my life has improved dramatically. So, here are my stories of facing my fears. I started to run at my fears instead of running from them. And if I can do it, so can you! So, Why Not Today? Start facing your fears and begin chasing your dreams.

2 MY FIRST FEAR

"Never be afraid to try something new. Remember, amateurs
built the Ark, professionals built the Titanic."
—Unknown

As I've said, I was fearless as a kid. Sure, I was occasionally scared of the
dark and definitely afraid of aliens after watching the movie E.T., but
aside from what my awesome imagination could dream up, I was fearless
most of the time. Nothing could stop me from flying, fighting, running
fast, jumping my bike, riding my skateboard, talking to strangers, or
selling candy door to door—nothing like that was scary at all. But I do
remember the first time I got really scared. It only lasted a short time but
it was a doozie. It's safe to say that event is burned into my mind forever.

At 4 or 5 years old, being one of the luckiest kids in the world, my
mother was a stay-at-home mom and my dad only worked during the
weekdays. In order to make ends meet my mom would babysit and watch
many other kids around the neighborhood so that other parents could
work to pay their bills. It was a win-win situation for everyone, and
especially me, because there was a house full of kids to keep company
with every day! This meant endless hours of playtime, fort building, and
game playing with lots of friends.

My parents bought a large Dodge passenger van. The van was
maroon and seated 8. That way, when Mom needed to go somewhere she
could haul all of us kids around with her. My family consisted of my
mom, my dad, 2 younger brothers, and an older sister.

At the time, my sister was taking accordion lessons. Yes, the big air-filled piano-like thing that you can walk around with and play. It was a very colorful pearl white swirled with all the other colors in the rainbow reflected in its shiny finish. Emily loved her accordion and was always playing it. Since she was taking lessons across town, we'd all load up in the van, take her over there and drop her off. Then Mom would take us to a park nearby, and we'd play for the half-hour that my sister had her lesson.

This unforgettable day began no differently. We had just dropped off my sister at her lesson, and were headed down the road towards the park in the big maroon van. All of us kids were chattering and laughing, the sun was shining, the air was warm and it just seemed like the perfect day. I remember this part so very clearly, because fear has a funny way of making you remember things.

As we rounded the corner onto a busier road, my mother suddenly sped up, then pulled over to the curb. As we looked where my mother was looking, we saw a young woman with long brown hair running from house to house. She was screaming and banging on doors! My mom opened the passenger window and yelled out, "Are you OK?"

The woman ran to the van as fast as she could and jumped inside. Trying to catch her breath she yelled, "He's trying to kill me! Drive!"

My mom stepped on the gas and we pulled away from the curb at what seemed like 100 miles an hour. This was before seat belts were common practice so you can imagine us kids hanging on for dear life. There was panic and commotion from the front seat. My mom was just driving, and the lady passenger was in hysterics. She kept saying it over and over. "He's going to kill me; he's going to kill me; he's going to kill me."

All of us kids didn't know how to act. We were so quiet, and so scared. What was going to happen now?

My mom looked over at the woman as she kept driving. "Who is going to kill you?"

"He is chasing me right now," she answered.

We looked out the back window of the van, and there it was—an old rattletrap four-door car weaving in and out of traffic, clearly chasing us down the road!

My mom looked at the panicked woman and said, "I have kids in here. I have to drop you off somewhere."

Mom was speeding, but driving as well as she could while being chased by a maniac who was going to kill this woman in the van with us. He's going to kill me—that's what we heard over and over.

There was no help from anybody on the road. I don't know if other cars could tell something was wrong. It was a duel between us and the crazy man, and he didn't show any sign of giving up.

So the cat-and-mouse game continued, block after block. I didn't know what I could do to help my mom! We were all so worried. Some of the kids were crying and the rest of us were being silent. This was a scary time and we had no idea how it would end.

After being chased by this old car for what seemed like several miles my mom whipped into the nearest gas station. All of us felt better, as if help was going to be right there.

Mom looked at the lady. "Go in there and get help!"

The woman jumped out of the van and ran inside, but before we could pull out into traffic here she came again! As she jumped in our van and locked the door she yelled, "I told the clerk to call the police, but I think it's safer in the van."

I could picture the police driving up and the lady getting out of the car, but that's not what happened. As we sat there waiting for the police, that old four-door tan heap of rust and dents came barreling into the parking lot as fast as it could. Tires screeched on the pavement and the car bounced from the weak shocks as it whipped in front of our van and turned sideways like on a cop show.

"Get on the floor! Get under the seats!" yelled my mom. Mom had locked the doors and kept yelling for us to get down. We were all crying at that point and huddled behind the back seats of the van, getting as far away as possible from our passenger, who kept yelling and pleading, "Please don't unlock the doors!"

All we could think about was fear and we weren't really thinking, but simply feeling terror! I was scared for my mom. My mom was in the front of the van and she was in danger as well. My mom was so upset that we could all feel that danger in the air.

The car door flew open, and this longhaired scraggly-looking man ran up to our van. "Open the door! Open the door!"

He was beating on the passenger window and the door itself, and pulling on the outside handle. "Open the door or I'm gonna break the window!"

The man's face was twisted and furious, and he was yelling at my mom that "she better unlock the door," while our passenger was sobbing "he's going to kill me!"

She was so sad and so scared. The lady was holding onto the door handle with one hand and holding the lock down with the other. She was shaking and crying, and obviously in fear for her life.

My mother was very upset, but she stayed calm. She said over and over, "The police have been called." And she said, "I am worried about the kids. I am worried about my kids. He's going to hurt the kids; I have to help my kids."

The lady kept screaming he was going to kill her, and the man was hitting the window so hard it sounded like it was about to break into a million pieces. So, we are sitting in the middle of a gas station parking lot with a maniac blocking our van full of kids, and causing a huge scene. There were two girls working inside the gas station. They were watching out the windows but you could tell that they were scared as well, and they couldn't help. We were waiting for the police but where were they? They surely were not arriving soon enough.

Outside the van, separated from us by a thin sheet of window glass, the man was now yelling that he had a gun in his car, and, "That van better be unlocked by the time I count to 3!"

My mom faced the crying woman. "Please, open the door. I'll tell the police his license plate and description. I'll wait and talk to the police—but I can't risk my kids."

The crazy man started his countdown. He slammed his fist against the window, yelling, "That's 1!"

Panic was rising in the lady passenger as well as in my mom. They were both pleading with each other, like two people in a lifeboat with a sea monster trying to rip his way in. The man slammed the window again—"That's 2!"

My mom's face was full of pain. She said, "I am so sorry; I have to protect my kids!"

As the maniac's fist slammed into the window one more time, we suddenly heard the unmistakable sound of the door handle being pulled, and the door lock popping open. The lady had listened to my mother's pleas and opened the door to her unknown future. My mom cried as the passenger door flew open, and there was one last loud scream from our passenger as the man pulled her out of our van—by her hair.

Everyone watched as he dragged her kicking and screaming across the parking lot and threw her into his car. He stomped on the gas and peeled out onto the street, disappearing around the corner.

Now everything was silent. All of us kids were still huddled on the floor behind the back seats, and my mom just sat there without speaking. We wondered if it really was all over, and just then the police pulled into the parking lot in 2 separate police cars. They had ended up going to the wrong gas station; that's what took them so long.

My mom was very shaken, but she gave the police a description and license plate number. I was looking at the lights flashing on top of the police vehicles and thinking about what had just happened. It seemed like a part of someone else's movie, but it had happened to us.

After the police had gotten our information, we drove home in silence. No one cried; no one spoke. We didn't see that tan car again, and we never found out what happened to that poor lady that day.

Mom calmed us by saying that she believed they were a married couple, or a boyfriend and girlfriend who were just in a fight. She said that the police had found them by now, and that they were probably not fighting anymore. That did make us all feel better, somehow. We had no choice but to hope and believe in the best outcome.

As the years have gone by I am thankful that my mother tried to help, and that she tried to keep us safe. My mom had been faced with a horrific decision. Nobody would ever want to be in a situation like that. That crazy car chase and abduction was my first time of being really scared in life. It wouldn't be the last.

3 LOSS

"Anyone who has lost something they thought
was theirs forever finally comes to realize
that nothing really belongs to them."
—Paulo Coelho

It seems like it was yesterday. It was around Halloween time, and I was 12 years old. My brothers and I were playing a game in the large family room while the TV provided some background noise. This was in one of the bigger houses we'd lived in growing up, a two-story house with a third-story game room for us kids.

My mother had been out of town because her dad, my grandfather, was very ill. Grandpa Elmer was a very strong man of few words, and he spent a good amount of time with me, even teaching me how to bowl at the local bowling alley during the summers of my youth.

Most early memories of Grandpa Elmer were of the many health problems he endured. You could tell he always had a lot on his mind.

Grandpa Elmer had this chair in his kitchen, right next to a window, where he would sit, drink his coffee, smoke his Pall Mall's, and read his magazines. He was a World War II veteran, and was into CB radios, camping, fishing, and hunting. He was a hard worker. Yes, he had his problems, but who doesn't? I still loved him very much—and he was my grandpa!

Well, Grandpa Elmer had fought severe arthritis and pain in his joints. He underwent many surgeries. He had lung and heart problems as well.

I still remember when the phone rang. This was well before cellular phones, caller ID, and the Internet. My dad called for me. "Eric, your mom wants to talk to you."

I ran into the kitchen and took the receiver. After asking my mom how things were going, her voice made it obvious that she was shaken up.

"Eric," she said, "go get an apple."

Well, we had apples at the house so I got one. She then proceeded to tell me to imagine that apple cut up into seven different pieces.

"Eric, picture that the apple is your grandfather's heart, and only one piece out of those seven are working."

I held onto the apple as if it were the answer to something.

"Eric, only 1/7th of Grandpa's heart is functioning right now. He is in congestive heart failure. Grandpa doesn't have much time left, Eric. He won't be coming home this time. I need to stay here, son, until Grandpa passes away."

This was very hard for me, being old enough to understand death, but never experiencing it. At this point nobody close to me had ever died. I was one of the very lucky ones who had four loving grandparents and two loving parents. No broken families, and no death. I had sort of thought that my life wouldn't involve those things.

"Eric, I'll call and let everyone know what's happening." She meant, as my grandfather got closer and closer to death. I passed the phone back to Dad and fell apart completely.

When Grandpa Elmer passed away, the family members who were there said it was a very emotional and beautiful experience, but we were all very lost and sad about it.

I'll always remember how sad my mom was after she came home. This was so heartbreaking for a kid my age to see. By witnessing Mom's sadness and pain my own feelings of loss were magnified. Seeing my mother like this hurt even more than when I'd been told that Grandpa Elmer had died.

Now it was time to go to the funeral. A funeral was an unknown thing for me, so I sure didn't know what to expect. Our family got in the van and drove for several hours to get to where my mom had grown up and where my grandparents lived. This was a small town in Northern Utah called Spanish Fork.

The drive felt very long but I was used to it over the years. It was always exciting to go see my grandparents, but not this day. When it was time for the viewing, to see my grandfather in his casket, I did not like it at all. It was nice to see so many of the cousins and family members I'd not seen in a very long time, but it was also a very bittersweet experience. All my aunts and my grandmother were sad and crying. There was just so much sadness and pain everywhere. A great many people filed in and out of the room to see my grandfather, offering condolences to the family. Everyone was sympathetic. I just remember the heavy feeling of grief.

The funeral was held the next day. We were all seated when a man came in and started to play the guitar. He sang about a dog named Shep, and everyone started crying hysterically at that point. Apparently "Old Shep" was not only one of my grandpa's favorite songs, but he used to sing it. Things were going downhill very quickly, and being a 12-year-old watching everyone fall apart, I wanted to do something, but there was nothing I could do. I had never seen sadness like this, and could not believe my grandpa was gone forever! I didn't know how to deal with any of this.

Then, the bombshell. They started to close the casket. My mom, my aunts and my grandma, all crying loudly, went up for one last look. Now even my dad started crying. Grandma was hugging and kissing my grandfather and crying so hard. My mom held his hand, and my aunts were hugging him, grasping every last second as the casket lid was lowered.

When the lid was finally closed, there was silence—silence broken only by sniffles and sobs from around the room. After witnessing such a dramatic and sad moment, I felt stunned and devastated. The sadness and pain was very overwhelming, and it just needed to be over.

Grandpa was gone. Would it be possible to ever feel happiness again? At the time, it seemed as if my normal life was lost forever. This whole day was one of sadness, fear, and loss. Not much was said on the trip home, and my mind was having a very hard time processing what had happened. Would life ever be the same? Would I ever find happiness again? Would my parents ever be happy?

Then realization kicked in. It was all clear now. Someone very dear to me was now lost—but what about all the other people close to me? As much as I loved Grandpa Elmer, we weren't nearly as emotionally close as my other three grandparents, and my parents! What was in store for me if anyone else died?

That was clearly the beginning of my fear of loss. To this very day, it is still my number one fear. Since Grandpa Elmer passed away, I have lost two other grandparents, an aunt, and multiple other relatives. Investing my whole heart into my family, each death was very difficult.

Losing people to death is not easy. I don't go to many funerals because of how they make me feel. Not a day goes by that I don't think about those who have passed on. And so, what was the lesson in all of this?

Life is hard. We are all here to live one life. We have one chance. We are all going to die at some point. We are all going to come to the end of our lives, so we need to make the best of what time we have.

There are very hard days ahead, as well as very rewarding days, for all of us. We do have a choice to make. My choice is to fight for happiness. My choice is to remember the lives of my loved ones, and not dwell on the deaths. My choice is to live my life as an example to those following, and to those who paved the path for me. I love all my family and am so glad we are all living close to each other. There are many who don't have a close family. They can't relate to having so many loving family members in their lives. Those individuals suffer in a whole different way. They feel loneliness, and oftentimes regret. Does it hurt more to love and lose, or never to love at all? I would not trade the love of my family or the time we have together for anything.

My Grandpa Elmer.

4 BULLIES

"I would rather be a little nobody, than to be a evil somebody."
—Abraham Lincoln

When I was 7 years old my dad was offered a promotion at his job. This promotion would require that he move our family south, about 300 miles away from our home. He would oversee the building of a new location for the company, and then develop the business in a new market. Being very sad to leave all my friends and the only house I'd ever known, I remember crying and saying goodbye to my friends, especially the cute blond next-door neighbor girl named Leah, because we planned on marrying some day. Kid crushes, you know how they are. It would be very difficult to just leave all of this behind!

In early June, school was already out for the summer and it was very warm. We rode inside a camper shell covering the back of Dad's green truck all the way to our new home, and the warm summer heat made that camper shell feel like a toaster oven inside. We had 2 cats at the time named Puff and Patches. My job on the ride down to our new home was to keep them occupied.

After a very long drive, we arrived in the new town for a fresh start. While our new home was being built we lived in a small rental house near a forest and a river. This was a great place for a kid. Searching for frogs and critters in the swamps behind our house as well as building huts and the occasional tree house were some of my favorite things to do.

The area we moved to was just beginning a building boom, experiencing a tremendous population increase that would last for several years. Many outsiders were moving in just as we had, to make better lives for their families and take advantage of this period of economic growth.

I started at a little old school called East Elementary, and had to ride a bus for quite some distance to get there. Everybody was a new face of course, but quickly I started to latch on to a few new friends. I went to East Elementary for 2nd through 4th grade, even after our new home was finished. When a school was built closer to us, they transferred me to Bloomington Elementary for the 5th grade year.

My dad was trying to build houses and sell them to make money, but every time he built the new house, the building lot and material for the home had gone up too much in price for him to make any profit. We ended up moving two more times while my parents sold a house and built another home. This time, we moved into a very large, very fancy house. After this move, things began to change.

From 5th grade I moved to the Woodward "6th grade center," as it was called, since it held only 6th grade kids. For the first time, we learned how to move through several classes a day as they prepared us for middle school. Sixth grade was not too bad. I met a few new friends and started taking band class. When we had to decide between choir and band, band won out because I wanted to play the trumpet.

At the end of 6th grade they separated all of us into two different middle schools in our town. So, we said goodbye to many of our friends and after summer vacation went on to our new schools. I was lucky, or so it seemed at first, because I got the newer middle school. It was also the school my sister attended. But I am not going to lie, things changed very quickly. I'm still not sure if it was my imagination, or my circle of friends, or that I was a chatterbox of a talker, or what, but there seemed to be a target on my back from the first day.

The next two years were a blur. This was a hard time, and a lot of what happened has been suppressed. You see, we may have lived in a bigger house but we did not have money. My parents would buy me new shoes, but they had to come from K-mart or Payless. At this school, if you didn't wear certain things, or if you weren't athletic, you became a huge target. Cheap shoes got you laughed at and teased.

I shared a locker with a friend from my first elementary school. Jake was also being picked on and bullied pretty bad. He started to get in with the wrong crowd. For the most part, I was still a good kid and a rule follower. Ironically, this may have been another reason for being picked on.

One day I opened our joint locker, and along with my books was a huge stack of pornographic books and cigarettes! The other strange items in there must have been drugs, and it all had to belong to Jake! I stared in disbelief, closed the door, and stood there for a moment.

Our school did periodic scans for things like this, and that day they were getting ready to do locker checks. Because of what was in my locker I was terrified! When I asked Jake about it, he told me he was selling all those things to other kids to make ends meet, and he didn't intend on stopping. As the locker checkers got closer and closer to the scene of the crime, I got more and more nervous. This was going to get me in trouble and surely get expelled.

What to do? Protect my friend, or protect myself? What a horrible dilemma! My insides were jumping around with the stress, and at the very last minute I turned and walked to the principal's office. I blurted out what was in my shared locker, that the non-school items in the locker were not mine, and I did not want to get in trouble for it. They were very appreciative and went and removed the pornography, smokes, and drugs. I was issued a new locker, but never actually used a locker again.

As for my friend Jake—well, we were never very close after that. Jake continued down a different path and we just went in separate directions. We did speak every now and again, and he was a dear friend during the times we were getting along, but his choices from there on led him down a rough path. Jake went from rehab center to rehab center. There were multiple arrests for driving under the influence, theft, and a revoked driver's license. He went to juvenile detention, and ultimately wound up in state prison. In fact, Jake passed away in prison after many years of being locked up. He sent me a letter apologizing for all that had happened when we were kids. I was able to go and see him just before he passed away and I will always be grateful for that.

After the locker incident, the bullying got worse. At this school, kids would take ballpoint pens and stick a pin or needle where the ballpoint was. They'd push the clicker at the end of the pen so the needle would stick out, walk past and stab you with it. Yes, I got jabbed several times.

Things were so bad in 8th grade that I used to hide outside and eat lunch by myself. I always brought a sack lunch to keep with me and eat away from the other kids. One day while quietly sitting against a brick wall, eating my lunch in the sun and just relaxing with my eyes closed, a shadow suddenly blocked out the sun. As my eyes quickly opened, there stood JoAnne, one of the meanest tomboys in school. She had short black hair, wore dark lipstick, and dressed in goth style outfits with a chain on her pants. She had multiple piercings and just looked plain mean and angry, and she was staring at my lunch. I had a juice box, peanut butter and honey sandwich, some chips, and some cookies.

"You got anything good in there." It wasn't a question.

"No, just a sandwich and my lunch," I answered.

How could I get her to just leave? Truth be told, I was bigger than she was, but was just a big softie—a gentle giant, as my mother would always say.

"Well lemme see. I'm hungry." JoAnne bent down with her eyes on my food.

I was polite, but hungry too. "Well, this is my lunch and I'm . . . oww!"

JoAnne punched me hard in the stomach and grunted, "I wasn't asking."

She reached in the bag, pulled out my sandwich, and tossed the rest of the bag in my lap. She walked off, pants chain swinging. I felt so broken. Now I couldn't eat in the lunchroom for fear of getting picked on, or outside either?

Unfortunately, JoAnne stole my lunch more than once. After this first meeting, I learned to let her have what she wanted. I often thought about telling a teacher or someone, but knew it would make things worse by getting labeled a nark, someone who tattled on others.

5   IT GOT WORSE

I was one of the shy kids. After gym class, we hated to change and shower with all the others. The unembarrassed would run around, flick us with towels and laugh. One day, after running laps, everyone was either showering or dressing. The laughing and towel popping gave way to cries of "It burns! What's going on?"

Several boys kicked their clothes back off and tried to stop their skin from itching and burning. They were sure suffering, but I got dressed normally and lucked out—they didn't get me. Some 9th graders had come into the dressing room and sprinkled itching powder, the really irritating stuff you could get at the practical joke store in town, into some of the other kids' underwear and shorts.

The older kids came in, laughing and taunting us with what they'd done. One walked up to me. "You have something in your eye," he said, and reached over and wiped a finger full of IcyHot muscle rub right in my eye! He started laughing as if it were the funniest thing on the planet. The gel burned horribly and both my eyes were watering uncontrollably. I tried to wipe it away as the gang of 9th graders laughed hysterically and pointed at me, making sure everyone saw "the crying baby."

I was not crying though. My eye was just burning so bad. We looked to our gym teacher for help but he just laughed too. "Hey, boys will be boys!" He acted like it was just how things were supposed to be. Needless to say, the locker rooms were now avoided at all costs.

And how about the bus stop? Wow—let me say this was another nightmare. Multiple times kids threw rocks at me and laughed. Did I do things to deserve this? Maybe I was irritating or maybe sometimes weird, but the kind of anger being thrown at me was simply not justifiable.

On the bus, no one would ever let me sit by them. Every day I had to play the game of *can I get on in time to find a seat?* Then, how many people would I have to ask before I could sit down? How many before one said yes? After a while, I began to sit by this one older kid. He had been held back a few years and was in 9th grade at the time. He went by Curly, but his real name was a mystery. Curly was very big, very tough, and most important, he was not mean to me. Curly wasn't really nice to me either, but he did let me sit by him and he wasn't mean. Of course, nobody messed with Curly because he was so big.

Every day during this period of my life had the same relentless sameness. Certain kids would pick on me and laugh, throw rocks, call me names, and make life miserable. That same angry goth girl would steal my lunch, the same kids in the halls would stab me with their pen-and-needle shanks. I was so tired of this—just plain fed up! I'd had enough and it was time to stop.

So, I devised a master plan in my head on how to survive the rest of my 8th grade year. Surely when 9th grade began everything would be fine, and then I'd be big man on campus. I'd be an old 9th grader, almost grown up—I just needed to make it through the rest of this year.

A foolproof strategy came to mind. I was going to pay Curly, the big kid on the bus, to protect me. So one day I took all the change and money from my piggy bank to the bus stop. I waited through the usual jeers and outbursts from the kids. Climbing on the bus and finding my usual seat next to Curly, I got up the nerve to ask him.

"Curly, do you think you could be my bodyguard? I can pay you."

My breath was stilled as he sat silently for a moment and looked at me. The suspense was horrible! Then Curly spoke. "Are you serious? Fight your own battles."

The bus audience was also waiting for Curly's answer, because his decision was followed by howls of laughter as the other kids around us heard about my offer to pay him to protect me. This refusal was like another punch in the stomach. I really didn't know what to do, and was at the end of my rope. Curly had been my solution. How would I ever get through the rest of 8th grade?

Reaching home, the answer suddenly appeared quite clearly. Why hadn't I thought of this before? Since Curly wouldn't help me, there was no other choice but to stop going to school! Now, my parents would not go for this. The only way to manage it was to be sick. And I did feel sick—sick with anxiety and fear—so why couldn't I just stay home sick? The minute this decision clicked in my brain, the tension, worry, and fear was much less!

The next day at school found me headed to the office, sick to my stomach. The school nurse had me call Dad to come to the campus. He'd come pick me up in his green truck and take me home. And that's what happened. My stomach acted up a couple of times per week after that. Then, I just stayed home sick and missed many days. My mom tried to meet with the principle and to work out solutions to my obvious problem, but she could never get them to take her seriously.

Missing so much school, things were a little better for me. Church, on the other hand, had become a problem. Throughout 7th and 8th grade my bullying problems grew worse and worse, but mostly stayed contained within the school day. But suddenly things began to deteriorate quickly at church as well! Church is not a place you would expect to see much bullying, but it's just as real there as it is at school.

One particular Sunday, I was old enough to participate in a special religious ceremony we had in our church. Standing in front of all those people was going to be nerve-wracking, but now at 12 years old, it was very exciting to be part of it. There were two rows of kids about my age, and I was sitting on the front row. Unfortunately, some of the bully kids from school were also in my church congregation and yes, participating in this ceremony.

Getting ready to stand up, suddenly something splatted against the back of my head. It didn't hurt, but reaching back I touched a big glob of spit. The kid behind me was laughing, along with his friends. One of them said, "Now he has to go through this whole thing with spit in his hair!"

They laughed and laughed, and they were right—that spit was in my hair the whole time. It was embarrassing and humiliating. Of course, nobody noticed that spit glob, but it was there, and I knew it. The minutes that passed felt like hours. As soon as the meeting was over I went into the bathroom and wiped out the spit. That day was very hard. Was there no refuge even in the house of God? After that, I rarely participated in that ceremony.

During Sunday school, we'd study scriptures with kids our age and the teacher. Well, as far as bullying goes, Sunday school was beginning to feel like real school. One Sunday, entering the classroom after most of the class was already seated, I sat in one of the few chairs left over, and within seconds my nose started burning with a horrific smell of sulfur and rotten eggs! The kids were all laughing, but why?

The smell was coming from the floor, and looking down, there were small bits of broken glass all over the carpet. Oh no—a stink bomb! You could buy these little glass vials that were full of a terrible smelly substance. They had placed the stink bomb under the leg of this chair, and when I sat down the glass broke and it started stinking. Yes, it made it look like the smell was coming from me.

The bombing ended up being a little worse than expected because we had to evacuate our class, and even several classes around us. When the leaders found out what had happened they tried to find who was responsible, but the perpetrators never would fess up. To this day it's a mystery as to who did this, but it was probably the same kids who spit on me a few weeks before.

As far as I was concerned, my life was officially ruined. Since turning 12 my life had been completely the worst. In fact, it seemed that life could not possibly get worse! There was really no end in sight.

Then one day, the time had come—I made it to summer! Made it to peace, and no more bullying. This was surely a day to celebrate!

Summer started off great. There was Wes, a new kid who moved into our neighborhood, and I immediately tried to make friends with him. We decided to explore some of the rock trails on the hill by my house.

Heading for the hill, we passed a large group of kids playing by the park. Unfortunately they began to shout things at us, and Wes said something in response. Whatever he said is lost in time, but it made them all very angry, very fast, and they began to stampede our way! Wes ran like the wind in the direction of his house. I was slower and not very athletic, and got separated from Wes, somehow ending up going the opposite direction.

With the angry gang in pursuit, I headed toward the golf course in hopes that maybe a golfer or some other adult would see and help.

Outnumbered and very scared, I ran all the way down to that golf course but didn't see anyone! The pack was still following, so I headed for the clubhouse, running across the fairway and aiming for a stream that was protected by lots of trees. Pushing into the thick greenery, I hid under a tangle of branches. Peering out of the thicket onto the fairway, my eyes scanned where the other kids should be showing up any second now.

Concealed by the trees, my breath was going in and out like my sister's accordion while my brain wondered how to get out of this mess.

And then there they were! The idea of a golf course slowed them somehow, because the mob of kids was now *walking* down the dirt hill and onto the side of the fairway.

Then a voice crackled from a loudspeaker at the clubhouse. But instead of announcing a golfer about to tee off, a man boomed, *"Hey, kid hiding in the river, get outta there!"*

My cover was blown, and the angry kids knew exactly where I was!

There was no choice now but to come out and take whatever they thought I deserved. With head hung low I crossed the fairway back towards the group of kids.

One of the boys was very round, plump, and tall and seemed to be the leader of the group. He had grease stains on his shirt that was just a little too tight and small for his body. Then another was tall and skinny and had spiked hair and freckles. They were a very diverse and different group of kids, but they all seemed to have one common goal—to beat me up.

I looked at the mob and said, "I'm sorry. Please don't beat me up."

One kid walked over to me. He didn't look threatening at all, but acted like he was going to shake my hand—and then he pushed me. One of the other kids was kneeling behind me because I went backwards over him.

When I hit the ground the beating began. Several of them surrounded me and started hitting and kicking. It seemed like a few minutes when one kid start suddenly yelling at the others to stop. He even cried! Someone was defending me—I was so happy! I didn't know him, but he kept crying, pleading and pulling on guys' arms until the rest of them stopped attacking.

As the mob of kids walked leisurely away, my new friend Jared helped me up off the ground. He walked back to my house with me and apologized the whole way. I never told my family what happened, because that would just mean more worrying. Being chased for some distance and then attacked was an incredibly scary thing.

The names of those kids who attacked me? I can't tell you, but I can tell you the name of the boy who stood up for me. I will always be grateful to Jared for taking a stand. Later, I realized that during the beating or after, there was not another word from the voice of the loudspeaker. This whole event would have been clearly visible from the clubhouse.

As for Wes, the new kid in the neighborhood—I never talked to him or even saw him again! What happened or where he ended up is not known. Maybe he just kept running, like Tom Hanks in *Forrest Gump*.

The rest of that summer was fairly quiet and uneventful. Maybe that last incident was the end. I truly hoped that the bullying days were now past.

6 THE DAY THAT CHANGED MY LIFE

"What if the kid you bullied at school, grew up, and turned out
to be the only surgeon who could save your life?"
—Lynette Mather

Other than the golf course attack, there were no more problems with
bullying during the summer. Ninth grade was coming up, but it would be
great because I would be one of the older kids on campus. It would be my
turn to help initiate those young 7th graders and teach them the ropes. I
would finally be popular, and had definitely paid my dues. I had kept a
few friends over the years, and this year would start off right. My mom
even went out and bought a nice pair of expensive Nike Air Jordan shoes
so there'd be no teasing about my low budget clothing.

Entering the 9th grade very optimistically, with only one more year
in middle school, I was ready to be top dog with all the other 9th graders.
Things were going great, and school was actually fun. And some of my
grades were beginning to improve. It's true—my grades were not good at
all since I missed so much school in 8th grade, and had barely passed my
classes. Despite grades, things were going as well as they ever had since
the 6th grade.

It was a nice fall day. Since we were technically considered
freshmen in high school, I had decided to go to a high school football
game with my friend Randy. This would be my first high school football
game, and there was excitement in the air. It was also my big sister's
school, and she was a senior. Though Emily would be there at the game

with her friends, I didn't really hang out with her much. Emily was very popular, and friends with all the jocks and the drama people. Somehow she could be friends with anyone, and never experienced my problems.

Well, about halfway through the game Randy and I decided it was time to go. Back in those days we didn't have cell phones, so we were going to walk to a gas station up the road and use the pay phone to call my mother to come and get us.

In the crisp evening air, we headed up the road towards the station. There was a dirt trail nearby that would cut several minutes off our walking time, so we decided to take that shortcut.

The sun was setting with orange and red streaks as we started up the dirt path through dozens of large bushes and plants taller than we were. The trail was probably a good half-mile, and we were close to halfway through.

Suddenly, two guys stepped out of the bushes behind us, but we thought nothing of it at that point, since they were probably going to the gas station as well. But really, they didn't have the look of someone just headed to a gas station. They looked like they had something else in mind.

Randy and I began to pick up the pace, but within a short time the bigger boys were practically right on our heels. They were so close we heard their feet slapping the dirt. They were gaining on us! One of them mumbled something, and I turned my head to look.

This was a mistake, as one of them shouted, *"What are you looking at?"*

As I turned away from them there was a heavy blow to the back of my head. I pitched forward into the dirt and out of the corner of my eye saw Randy running away as fast as he could!

This was big trouble—flat on my face in the dirt in the middle of a field covered in greenery, a place where nobody could see or hear anything. These were two very big and very angry guys, and one had just punched or kicked me in the back of the head. There was a second of total stillness, but then both began to punch and kick me.

"No, stop! Oww, no!"

I cried and screamed, but they would not stop. Blow after blow and kick after kick, I tried to protect the core of my body by curling up in the fetal position on my side. My head was pounding and my eyes were filled with dirt and tears. As bad as the pain was, it was *my fear* that was getting the best of me.

This is it, I'm going to die. The thought was very matter-of-fact. This was going to be the end of it for me.

These guys pounded on me for what seemed like several minutes. And maybe they had a knife or a gun as well. Would they kill me and then steal my wallet? There was $60 in that wallet, and it was all I had. My life was important, but I sure did not want them to know about that money. But how long could they beat me like this? Fighting back might just get me killed quicker.

I didn't know what to do, only to just lie there and take it. Then one said, "I think he's had enough."

"OK—just one more."

The guy said it so calmly, it was like beating someone senseless was something he practiced every day of his life.

My hands were pressed against my face as the final blow smashed into the side of my head, right on the ear. There was a terrible ringing sound and immediate pain. With tears running down my grimy face and ears filled with dirt, I watched the two blurry figures walk slowly up the trail, as if they had no special place to be. Then, nothing but birds chirping, and my sobs.

My damaged body stayed down on the dirt for what felt like the longest time. What had I done to deserve that? Not a thing! So my problems with bullying were not over. A thought surfaced in my mind—it was my life that was over! There was just no point in living anymore.

Finally I picked myself up and limped up the trail to the gas station. There was Randy, waiting anxiously. He'd been too scared to even come back and see what happened, but I don't blame him for running. Neither of us stood a chance against those guys. Randy was just as scared as I was.

There was no way to hide my injuries, so when Mom arrived to pick us up, she was very upset! She could not believe what had happened, and I could tell that she was just done with all of this.

Going to school the next day, the news of my beating had spread quickly across campus. People were laughing at me and pointing. There was a rumor that those kids were going to make my life miserable throughout the rest of my school days. Hearing this, I'd never been more discouraged or scared. There was no hope at all. What could anyone do?

To their credit my parents *did* go to the school to address this attack, but the school seemed to think it was not an issue! There were multiple failed attempts to meet with school staff to fix the problem.

One day after school Mom and Dad pulled us all together to make a big announcement. They were not happy with the school and how they were treating the bullying situation, so within days of the attack they put the house up for sale and moved us to a rental house, and a new school.

My parents were so worried about me that they were willing to do anything to make my life better. They were also worried that the same things could happen to my younger brothers, who were just about to enter the same middle school.

So, we packed up and moved out. I really didn't know what to expect as we moved to a new school, new neighbors, and a new life in a new part of town. We would now live in a very small house, in a very humble part of town.

It was scary to try this new school, partly because I'd never experienced coming into a school almost at midyear as the new kid. This school would be new to me as a student, but as a building it was old and very rundown. And I remember thinking to myself, *I can never let them see me as a victim again.* I'd even be a bully if necessary, just to survive at this new school.

But thankfully, that's not what happened. There was only pure acceptance. Within the first few days of living in our new house I met a kid my age. His name was Tony, and we quickly became friends. Then Tony's friend John became my friend! I had not known this feeling since being a little kid. This was amazing—going to this school I already had some friends from the neighborhood!

At this school, the other kids didn't wear fancy clothes or name-brand shoes. It was a completely different experience. I was so happy to be able to wear normal shoes. And I began to make friend after friend. The difference was unbelievable.

Yes, I was very cautious not to let on that I was bullied at my other school. That was my secret. And I made sure not to do anything that would draw attention to me. That feeling was never again going to be part of my life! In fact, I was cautiously guarded for the rest of my school years. But I loved my new school, and made some good friends!

From 9th grade to graduation were the best school years of my life. Never again did I sit alone at lunch; never again did someone beat me up. Bullied? Never again. My life was changed for the better. I didn't really dwell on those years of hell that I had endured, but I'll always remember the feelings. My mind constantly remembers different things that I had forgotten for a while. I learned a lot from those days, and today I would not trade them. I have forgiven all of those who beat me up, spit on me, threw rocks, or laughed.

There are times in my life where I may have even tried to be a bully out of survival. I recall once right after changing schools and trying to be tough. To avoid being seen as the weak new kid on the block that everyone could start picking on again, I tried pushing another kid around a few times, and felt so horrible that I later apologized, and that was the last of it!

All of us are bullies at some point, as we learn how to go through life. There were times in my childhood where I may not have been the kindest to other kids as well. There are many regrets from my past, but there is nothing I can do to *change* the past. However, by sharing my story and helping others, I have been able to let the past go, and that is an important part of my life.

These experiences taught me at an early age about depression and anxiety. I would even come to find out what severe depression is, and I have dealt with this many times over the years. I became very guarded, and it was hard for me to make friends at times. Yet I would not trade those days for anything because of the lessons learned, and the person I have become.

We are all bullied in some way or form at some point in our lives. We all develop fears because of this, and put up walls that are sometimes very difficult to break down! Many of us are ashamed of such experiences, but I am not ashamed at all. I am proud of who I am and what I've been through—and you should be proud of you, too! As you read deeper into this book, you will learn some of the ways I was able to fight back and overcome. You will see that there is a solution to breaking free from the past that holds you down.

For many years I wondered why those bullying experiences were part of my life. As my musical career turned more toward speaking and working with the youth on bullying, the realization came to me—these experiences were necessary so that I could truly relate to some of the challenges that many of us have faced.

What I looked like at that awkward age.

After moving to the better school I ended up getting
my Eagle Scout rank, and so did both of my brothers.
(The quality is very low on my old scanned photos.)

7 BIG GREEN

From as early as I can remember, my dad drove around in Big Green. Big Green was a green 1978 Ford F150 short box, single cab, Ranger Edition, 4x4 truck. This truck was one of my favorite things in my life. You see, being as much a daddy's boy as a mama's boy, I loved to watch Dad drive around in his big truck. Since it was only a single cab, and not having the car laws we do for kids today, I always got to ride up front with him.

Dad always had the same pine-scented Christmas tree air freshener hanging from his lighter plug. Inside the ashtray was always a package of my favorite chewing gum, a mint gum in little cube shapes. When you chewed on them, a sugary minty gel squished out. I loved to help myself to Dad's mint gum.

This truck was always spotless, and kept neat inside as well. Behind the bench seat were all kinds of fun things. Dad had his spotlight, jumper cables, .22 rifle that my grandpa gave him, tools, emergency road flares, a tow chain, gloves, and much more. Dad was always prepared.

Camping, fishing, chopping wood, and going to the family ranch in Bear Valley were just some of the things we did. Dad had a pickup shell that would cover the bed of the truck, so all of us kids could ride in the back. There were so many adventures in Big Green.

Driving down the freeway in a snowstorm, Dad would often stop to pull cars out of trouble and back onto the road with his tow chain. In our travels, he stopped to help people many times along the way, and sometimes this made for long trips. My dad could do anything, and so could his truck!

Turning 16 and finally getting my driver's license, I'd always take Big Green when Dad would let me borrow it. There was a little hatchback car that our family bought for my sister, but she didn't need it anymore, and I sure did not like driving it. For one thing, as a very tall and bigger kid, it was just not that comfortable.

I tried to learn everything possible about Dad's truck. Like most kids who are into cars, I grew to know what was so awesome about it, including the big block 400 cubic inch motor. It had dual shocks per wheel for off-roading. It had super low 4:11 gears and a posi-trac rear differential. When you locked the front hubs to put it in 4-wheel drive, you had a locked front and rear differential, and with that low gear ratio you could climb anything in this truck. I'd challenge my friends to races, off-road contests, and different climbing challenge events. There was just something special about driving Dad's truck and having so many memories of it throughout my entire life.

One day while driving across town in Big Green, I decided to race the car next to me at a stoplight. We both revved our engines and I power braked the truck. Power braking is when you hold your foot on the brake and push the gas, so that the back tires will spin and smoke.

When the light turned green, away we went!

Just a little ways up the road, Big Green was in the lead and I was already congratulating myself. Then, BOOM! A loud explosion went off from under the hood and Big Green's roaring engine went silent. The guy we'd just outrun passed me by, and I coasted off down a side street. Oh no—what had I done to Big Green! And what was Dad going to say?

I walked up the road and found a phone, calling Dad to come help. At this point in my life, the actual mechanics of fixing the truck was not my thing. Dad came right over, but I didn't mention the stoplight race.

We tried everything to get the truck running, but had to have it towed to a shop. When the shop called us, it was bad news. That engine was blown. A cam had snapped and messed up all the valves. This would be a very costly repair, and Dad was not happy with me at all. Big Green was his baby. In the first place, he'd leased this truck to be able to afford it, and then after the lease was up he got a loan to buy it. It wasn't easy for him to buy this truck, and he loved it.

It was painful to see the disappointment on Dad's face. I had to handle this problem, and since I'd been working some odd jobs and taking care of other people's yards for money, I could pay for a new engine. "And Dad," I asked, "would you actually sell Big Green to me?"

Dad ended up talking to a friend of his and found a rebuilt 400 cubic inch small block engine that would fit in our truck. Dad's friend offered to install the engine for us and get it all running again for $2,000.00.

Dad looked at me and said, "Eric, I'll pay for the engine, and if you pay me $100.00 per month until that engine is paid off, I'll consider Big

Green to be your truck."

Well, to me this was a total steal! Not only would I own the truck of my childhood and entire life so far, but it would also have a new engine. That was really exciting!

Dad's friend put in the new engine and it ran like a champ, even faster and more powerful than before! Over the next few years I added upgrades, including big tires, souped-up exhaust and emission systems, and a roll bar. I installed an awesome custom sound system with subwoofers behind the seat. I got a CB radio, and would drive around talking to truckers and other people I'd meet who had CB's. We even had a club for the locals who used CB's.

My buddies and I would always take my truck camping and fishing, since it could go up any Jeep trail you threw at it. I can't even remember half the places we went in this truck. It was just such a fun vehicle, filled with memories. We'd take Big Green on some sort of an adventure almost every weekend.

It *was* an older truck and it did continually have various problems, but Dad helped me work on making modifications and doing repairs. Many nights and weekends we'd be in the garage doing some type of work. We rebuilt the carburetor a few times. We changed radiators, starters, alternators, and one time even tackled a timing belt change. Most of this truck had been rebuilt at this point. There was a small issue with the flywheel, and the distributor needed to be changed, but we were not ready to tackle that just yet!

This truck was my life. I drove it all through high school and into my first year of college. My friends all loved my truck too, and everyone recognized us driving around because of how it stood out. Big Green was a big part of our lives. But things were about to change, and real fast. Over the next few weeks I would learn some very valuable lessons.

It was October, and the traditional Deer Hunt was rapidly approaching. My dad, brothers, and friends would always go deer hunting. It was a very important tradition to all of us, handed down from both of my grandparents, and from theirs before that. I remember many hunts with Dad and my grandpa, and we always had Big Green with us.

One year with my dad, my brothers, and Grandpa Dodge, Big Green got a flat tire up by our family ranch. Dad had a lock on the spare tire so nobody could steal it. Well, now we needed that spare, and he'd lost the key to the lock! It was snowing, and I remember Dad under the truck in the snow for what seemed like hours, banging on the padlock and trying to break it. Luckily, my grandpa had his truck with him as a backup, or we'd have been in big trouble out there.

After the longest time, Dad broke the lock. We got the spare off and guess what? It ended up being flat as well! This was not a good day for us. Dad was muddy, and we were all cold and stranded in the hills. So, we crowded into Grandpa's truck and took off to a nearby town where we found a tire of the right size, and finally got Big Green moving again. There are many memories like this. Big Green was a very temperamental vehicle, but I sure loved it.

This particular Thursday in October was no different than any other. Big Green was all tuned up and ready for the hunt. My friend Jason and I decided we wanted to go spot-lighting to see if we could find any big, huntable bucks out on a local popular hunting area called Utah Hill. And when we say *hill*, it's more like a mountain. We both had jobs and school the next day, so we decided to head out early and reach a place called Horse Canyon. We'd get there about dark and begin spotlighting on the way back home. It was a good 90-minute-plus drive out there that included 30 miles of dirt road behind a mountain on the Utah/Arizona border. We stopped at a local store, grabbed a Gatorade and a bag of beef jerky, and headed out for the evening.

The sun began to set as we drove around to the back side of the mountain. We were winding and turning for the longest time down that narrow dirt road, lined with countless thousands of Joshua cactus trees. We jumped a few deer on the way, but knew we'd hit the jackpot once we got up into Horse Canyon.

About five miles from Horse Canyon there's a large water tank. The cattle rancher who owns the tank was known for putting goldfish in it to keep the moss down. Jason was telling me about how big some of these fish were getting. We were both big into fish and had fish tanks, raising many types of fish at that time. I asked Jason if he wanted to stop and check it out, and he was happy to do so. Pulling up next to the tank, we left Big Green running. It was almost dark by this time, so I left the headlights on and we used a flashlight to look down into the tank and see those giant goldfish swimming around.

It was really only a few minutes, but when we turned back to my truck my heart suddenly sank. Those headlights were looking very dim! This was not a good sign, and I knew exactly what it meant—the truck alternator was failing, and Big Green was running on straight battery power.

"Oh no, the battery! Jason, we're in big trouble!" Running towards

Big Green and looking over at Jason, he seemed as worried as I was.

I began to panic. We were 30 miles from any paved road, there was not another single living soul around, and—the big AND—I didn't tell anyone where we were going. Nobody knew where we were.

"Jason, get in, we've gotta go now!" And I floored that truck, racing back towards town as fast as possible.

Jason braced himself with his feet on the floorboard and one hand on the dash. "Calm down Eric, calm down! It won't do us any good if you kill us on the way home."

"Look Jason, there's no way anyone is gonna find us out here on this mountain!"

I kept driving furiously, keeping it between the ditches, as they say, but within a few miles my headlights had failed completely. The battery just couldn't keep them lit.

Jason was holding a flashlight out the passenger window, so at least part of the road was visible. The engine was still running, but not very well. The dual exhaust pipes that were recently added began to backfire, and kept shooting flames out of both sides of the truck. We had only moments before the engine would stop for good, and I was determined to reach the junction where this dirt road met another that was a little more traveled. That was our only hope of being found.

No lights at all now, and the engine was stumbling and running rougher. We swung around one more horseshoe turn, going as fast as the truck could go without sliding off, and the engine shut down. That quietness was a sick feeling. We coasted down the hill as far as we could, and rolled the truck right onto the main junction I had hoped for. We sat there in silence for a minute and then began to try and get the truck running.

Remember, there were no cell phones at the time. There was no way to let anyone know where we were, and that we were all right. I was so upset—how could I not have told anyone where we were going? Why was I not more prepared? After all, I was an Eagle Scout! The motto is "Be Prepared," but that day I was as far away from *prepared* as we were from home.

We tried to start the truck for a few hours but all attempts were unsuccessful. I finally had the brilliant idea to use the CB radio and call for help! Maybe we could reach a truck driver to get word to my parents that we were OK.

This would work! I keyed the mic and called for help in the darkness—with no success whatsoever. No one could hear us. I used what little battery power there was for the truck spotlight, and flashed S.O.S. in Morse code up at the planes occasionally flying over.

I was so concerned about the worry this would cause my parents, and was desperate to get word to them somehow. Rummaging behind Big Green's bench seat I found the old road flares that Dad had put there. We quickly lit them up out on the dirt road behind the truck.

Then Jason mentioned a ranch he knew of. It was about 10 miles away, and we could walk there! Surely someone was there who could help us.

One thing about being stranded in the wilderness, there are plenty of rocks available, so we constructed giant rock arrows on the road showing the direction we were walking. If someone came upon our truck they'd know which way we went. We left the flares burning on the road with the directional arrows.

That flashlight we'd been using for a while also ended up running out of power, and we were now completely in the dark. October in Utah—it was getting very cold and we didn't have any jackets or coats. How are we going to keep warm? We decided to run all the way to the ranch so we could get there sooner. We were not able to see very well, but could tell we were still on the road since we weren't running into trees or rocks.

We ran for the longest time. At one point we stopped for a break, our breath going frosty in the cold night air, and could hear coyotes howling all around us. It was an eerie feeling. No vehicle, no gun, no flashlight, no way to get help, and miles away from anything.

We kept running and finally got close enough to see the ranch in the darkness. "Eric, we're in luck," Jason panted.

Something didn't look quite right though, as we quickly realized that nobody was there! This ranch had no phone or power, no anything, and we were not in luck at all.

We didn't pursue going all the way to the ranch house, since we hoped that the truck would eventually start back up after it sat long enough, or that someone would come along that dirt road and find Big Green. We decided to make the trek all the way back to the truck to wait for help, or at least wait until morning.

The night air was like ice and we were freezing! There were some big game cloth wraps behind the seat in case we got a deer in the coming weeks, so we wrapped up in those stretchable cloths and got inside the truck. There was a little Gatorade left and a bit of jerky that we rationed throughout the night.

Have you ever been too cold to sleep? We both were, and didn't sleep a bit. Seeing the twinkling stars in the black sky above was beautiful, but we were too distracted by the cold to fully appreciate it at the time.

Also, what was this was doing to our families? Never before had I not been home at a decent hour, especially on a work or school night. Unlike poor Big Green, my mind was going a thousand miles an hour. We called for help on the CB and continued the S.O.S. spotlight flashes throughout the night.

We had hours to plan our next move as we sat shivering in the game bags, and decided to head towards the main highway on foot as soon as the sun started to rise. This would take many miles of walking and several hours. We were both tired, cold, hungry, thirsty, and by now both of our families would be completely in chaos! I knew that my own family was certainly thinking the worst. We were OK, we were fine—but we couldn't tell them.

When the sky finally began to lighten, we climbed out of Big Green and walked as fast as we could for hours. We just ignored our thirst and put one foot in front of the other, but we weren't very talkative by that point. Finally we saw a truck headed toward us down the dirt road. We ran towards it, waving our arms to flag him down, and I cried with relief all the way to that truck.

Jason yelled out, "That's my dad, we are saved!"

It was indeed Jason's dad. This was a miracle. As he pulled up to us, he smiled and said, "Looks like you boys could use some help!"

He drove us back to my truck and with some jumper cables, he got Big Green brought back to life. Without the strain of headlights and cargo lights, we were able to keep the motor running and headed back towards town. We hadn't asked Jason's dad how he found us, or what was going on. I was just desperate to get home and get the word to my family that I was OK. Already I'd missed work, school, and much of the day.

Since Jason had left his truck at my house, he ended up riding back with me instead of going with his dad. And as both vehicles made it out onto the highway, I remember flooring that green truck and flying as fast as I could for home.

Crossing the mountain range, I noticed a line of cars behind us and strangely, they were keeping up with us at 20 miles per hour over the speed limit!

Then a Suburban went to pass us. Glancing in the side mirror, I thought *this guy must be crazy*. The Suburban flew by like we were standing still and as he pulled in front of us, he hit his brakes! I stood on my brake pedal and somehow didn't hit him, while the Suburban came to a complete stop in the middle of the highway. Those other cars had all stopped behind us, so we were surrounded! Several guys got out of the lead vehicle and walked back towards us.

Now what was going on? We just had one hell of a night, and these guys were not making it any better.

I rolled down the window as the bigger of the guys walked up to Big Green. This guy glared at us with his hands on his hips. *"Are you boys lost?"* he barked.

"No sir, we're just trying to get home," I answered.

Looking at this fellow, I decided he was with the sheriff's department. And Jason apparently was going to let me do all the talking.

Then the deputy scowled, "Have you been out partying all night or something?"

"No, we haven't," I replied, and told him our story.

The deputy said that he was with search and rescue, and that they were all out looking for us!

Thankfully Jason's dad caught up to us since we were stopped in the highway, and verified our story of being broken down on Utah Hill. Jason's dad found us because he figured that we'd have gone to the closest place to see deer—and that was Utah Hill.

Then the rescuer said that my parents and siblings were at home, and that they'd be very happy to hear from me! He spoke into his police radio. "We have a green truck with two boys, and they were headed for home, driving very fast."

Jason then went with his dad, and I drove on alone. When I finally got home my family was in tears, and even Dad was crying. Because consistency was such a big part of my personality, and because I always let people know my whereabouts, that whole event was way out of character. I had never failed to be at work to unlock the door for the customers, and had never missed a day of college. Yes indeed, they had all thought the very worst—*maybe Eric had rolled his truck and was hurt, or even dead.*

Our adventure at Horse Canyon was a very stressful 24 hours. I'd never been happier to have a family who cared so much. My brother told me he had knocked and rang the bell at Jason's house until 4:00 a.m., when Jason's dad finally woke up and came to the door. When he learned what was going on, he promised to help find us when the sun came up.

My parents had also called the police. They weren't much help because they have to wait 24 hours, since most of the time the missing kids are just partying somewhere, or at a friend's house. If they just wait, the missing person usually comes home. But my mother was very persistent, and made them understand how out of character this was. She just pushed until they got ahold of search and rescue.

This experience and the emotions I felt are unforgettable. Physically, my legs were tired and stiff from all the miles we had walked and run. That day I also learned many lessons on preparedness.

After that very traumatic night, in the weeks to follow things went back to normal. Big Green went to the shop and ended up getting a new alternator, and we did go hunting. The deer hunt was awesome!

Maybe now it was time to change that distributor I'd been holding off on. Dad and I spent hours in the garage one night and changed it out. It was a huge project, but we set the timing with Dad's timing light and got it done. After that we took the truck for a spin, marveling at how well this new distributor made it run. This seemed to be the best Big Green had run in all its years.

And Dad had just bought a brand new version of Big Green. This was Big Yellow, the same exact model, with dual shocks, a short bed, and exactly the same—only 18 years younger. Now we had Big Green and Big Yellow.

After our test drive, we parked Big Green in the gravel in front of our house and went inside. Little did I know that would be the last time I'd ever see my truck again.

Next morning I was headed to a wedding rehearsal for my friend Barry. Walking out the front door I immediately noticed Big Green—or rather, noticed it was not in its parking place!

I went back inside, calling out, "Mom, Dad, where's my truck? Did you move it? Did you let someone use it?"

Neither of them had any idea where it was, so I figured one of my friends was playing a joke on me. A couple of girl friends from high school would constantly do things to my truck, and I'd retaliate and "decorate" or do something to their car. We had this game going on for years now, but this was elaborate even for them.

Surely someone just moved it around the block, but when I walked down the street it wasn't to be seen. Crossing the area where it had been parked, a shiny little piece of metal winked up at me from the gravel. I reached down, picked it up, and recognized it instantly. It was the door lock to Big Green. Someone had sheared it right off! This could only mean my truck had been stolen.

In the case of a missing vehicle, the police came right over. They could not believe a locked truck was taken in a residential driveway in such a busy part of town. They vowed to work hard to find Big Green. And I was just sick. Big Green was not just a truck, it had been part of my life since being born. How could it be gone?

I made flyers and posted them all over town. Every friend, family member, or acquaintance got a phone call or a visit. Surely a big green truck would be easy to spot. The police said that most likely it was just taken for a joyride, and would soon be found out of gas somewhere.

I had high hopes that we'd find Big Green, but I ended up calling my friend Barry and bailing on his wedding! Besides the fact I didn't have a vehicle anymore, every minute was going to be spent looking for my truck.

As the hours turned to days, the days turned to weeks, and the weeks to months, my hopes of ever finding Big Green were diminishing. I was so sad and upset, and couldn't figure out how anyone could be this upset over a vehicle. After all, it was just a truck, so how could I feel this sad and hurt? Not to mention angry—I got so angry. Never in my life have I wished such harm as I did on those that stole my truck. I even imagined myself going back in time and hiding in the back of the truck with my rifle as they tried to steal it. Oh, the things I would do to those criminals! Just like being too cold to sleep when Jason and I were stuck, my anger was burning so hot that I couldn't sleep and I couldn't focus.

Many years have passed since then. And even though I purchased another truck, I continued to look for Big Green. Even today, I still chase down every truck that looks like it. I loved that truck, loved what it stood for, and still love the memories.

Unfortunately, a lot of us have experienced theft, and two of my mountain bikes had been stolen before Big Green was kidnapped, but never had I experienced this type of emotion. It did something to my ability to trust, and changed me. It has taken a lot of years to look back and not feel that anger. Still, I am very bothered when thinking of a person taking something that does not belong to them. Yet I have learned so much through all of this, and it's been a big part of my growth in life. So, I will always miss Big Green. It will always be my first truck, my dad's truck, and carry a whole lot of memories. Most likely I'll never see that truck again. Wouldn't it be cool though, if I did?

Big Green, parked right where it was stolen from.

8 THE SINGLE LIFE

"It is better to be hated for what you are
than to be loved for what you are not."
—André Gide, *Autumn Leaves*

This is a subject that is very personal to me. I have gone on dates with or
"dated" many different types of girls more than one time. I am very
guarded about my dating life, and I consider many of the girls that I went
out with to be wonderful friends. In this chapter, names will be changed
to protect people, as well as omitting many stories and details. But I do
want to make sure that you get a glimpse into my personal life because
it's very important in my journey.

My family raised me to be *a good kid*. I had good standards and
was—and still am—very reserved and shy when it comes to dating. Dates
were not allowed until at least age 16. That is, except for Leah, the 4-year-
old neighbor girl I proposed to and "married" when we were both 4! We
pretended to be boyfriend and girlfriend for years and years, and even
wrote letters to each other after our family moved away. It was a fun
childhood pretend romance, but it wasn't my first real dating experience.
Turning 16 was thrilling because now I could go on real dates. But I did
not know how to date, how to ask a girl out, or really anything about this.

There was a dance at my high school the April I turned 16. This was
my first opportunity to ask someone to go. None of my friends had asked
anyone to go, or had any idea what to do. I was not a popular kid, and
didn't really know anyone that I could ask. But there was this girl who
lived up the street from me named Amy and she went to my church on
Sunday. We always laughed and had fun at church. We didn't know each
other super-well since our family was new to the neighborhood, and this

was another new school for me. Yes, I was nervous, but I was going to ask her to the dance.

This occasion called for flowers, so I went to the store and bought some carnations. I didn't want to imply too much with roses, if you know what I mean. Walking up the path to her house and pacing back and forth for a few minutes, I was really nervous! My heart was pounding, and I finally walked to the door and knocked. Amy's dad answered. He was a very big guy, but luckily a nice guy.

"Is Amy here?" I asked. He kind of smiled and went and got her.

When Amy got to the door, I just mustered up the courage. "Would you like to go to the dance with me next Friday?" Those words went flying out as fast as they could go.

And she said YES. I was so happy! This would be my very first date. Amy and I did have fun at the dance. We had the giant school picture package taken, one set for each of us. Neither of us was popular and neither of us was considered *cool*, but we had a great time.

Intent on being a gentleman, I followed all the rules of getting doors, paying for dinner—all the things my parents taught me. It's been a long time since then, but all went well and we had fun at the dance—that will always be remembered. We remained friends for many years after this, and even went to our first college "girls ask guys" dance together, when Amy asked me to go.

During high school I pretty much went to every dance. Being in the marching band and drama crowd, we kind of had a group of like-minded students. We weren't popular, and we may have even been considered the nerds, but we were fine with that. At this new school we were a pretty large group.

Being way too scared of girls in high school, I never had an official girlfriend, but I did have a crush on Tammy, and she was great! Tammy was the lead in many of our musicals. Not only could she sing amazingly well, she could act. The first time I saw her on that high school stage, it was like her name was up in lights. I did everything to become friends with Tammy and get to know her. There was never a dull moment when she was around.

It was great to watch Tammy sing and perform, and we developed a great friendship. In 11th grade we went to junior prom together, and she asked me to Sadie's. We went on many dates and spent a lot of time together, even going to senior prom as well. We had so much fun!

Even though we never exclusively dated, you could say we were *kind of* dating. But we were both scared of each other, trying to be so proper and follow all the rules, so we never made it into that comfort

44

zone you need with someone you date. We were both so guarded, and I suppose you could say "ON"—being in *impress each other* mode all the time—that we never could break down those walls.

After graduation we both began to change quite a bit. Tammy went a completely different direction and we lost track of each other. Once in a while I'd hear about her or see her around, but we were now in college and the high school days were gone.

In college, life began to take a turn once again and I started to really struggle academically. Daytime I was working a job with my dad and squeezing in as many credits as possible in-between, on a half-ride band scholarship.

Reading music was not my strong point and I played mostly by ear. In high school it was always fun songs from movies and popular radio hits. Those were easy for me to copy by just listening to them, picking out the notes, and then memorizing the patterns. That skill worked out great in high school band, and that's how I won the scholarship.

Well, college was very different, and college symphony was a real struggle. They played difficult classical music like Mozart, Bach and Beethoven. Playing by ear was no longer cutting it, and it was painful. It would be horrible to be found out!

My other grades were slipping as well. I'd taken a few hard blows in English, barely getting a C-, while taking lots of science classes with plans to become a wildlife conservation officer. Originally, becoming a veterinarian seemed perfect, but hearing how many years of school were required, that idea was abandoned. There was no way I could make it 10 years!

So, one day in the geology class that all future wildlife conservation officers were required to take, my teacher asked us to stand up. He looked down at his desk, then up at us.

"Look around you. There are about 50 people in this class." He swept his arms out as if to enlarge the room. "Now imagine," he said, "that there were 100 people standing right here."

He paused for a moment as some of us looked around, almost expecting the extra 50 to appear at any time.

"OK, everyone sit down—except YOU." He pointed at a guy on the front row.

Still pointing at the student, our teacher then said, "One out of 100 will get a job as a wildlife conservation officer. One out of 100. You'd better be the best."

Oh, I felt sick all right. Failing music, failing English, and now officially informed that only *the best* would even have a chance at getting the job I wanted! At this time, depression and anxiety were already becoming a struggle. Socializing with people was difficult, and dating was a challenge as well. Things were not looking good. So I made a decision that day, and dropped out of college after just one year of school.

In my mind I was a complete failure. And back to bullying—here I was bullying myself pretty hard, but I didn't understand that at the time.

Despite being physically active, weight had been piling on since 10th grade, and now it was really picking up steam. Over the next few months my depression got even worse. I did enjoy working with my dad, but there was no dating and the only personal gains I could see were pounds of flab. My life was going nowhere. At least there were friends who'd go country dancing with me. We'd also go camping and fishing quite often.

My friends and I would go out to the Dance Factory on weekends and try to meet girls. All of us were kind of shy and reserved, so it took all we had to ask girls to dance with us. We'd dare each other and see who was brave enough to do this. One weekend Jason dared me to ask a really pretty girl to dance. She had boots, a cowgirl hat, and strutted around like she was pretty cool in general, and she *was* pretty cool in our eyes. We never talked to her, so we just called her "Eye Candy." That was just how us 19-year-old kids were, and that was our name for her. So one night, Jason dared me to ask Eye Candy to dance. Those butterflies were fluttering around in my stomach and my hands began to sweat, but I was going to do it—I could get through this! In my head I rehearsed just walking up and asking casually, *would you like to dance?*

The next song started off, and it was a slow number. This was my chance! Eye Candy usually got asked fast, so to be first required being close. I just jumped right over, smiled and asked, "Would you like to dance?"

She was always dancing with guys so I was sure she'd say yes. I was already trying to figure out how to keep the conversation interesting, as we'd be dancing for about four minutes. But wait—my focus came back quickly to Eye Candy. She had *not* said yes. What was taking so long?

Eye Candy looked at me, up and down, and then said, "UM, no thanks!"

Wow, it was like getting hit with a bat! She just flat turned me down. Then as quickly as she'd said no, she was asked by another guy, and they whisked past me out onto the dance floor.

All my friends were looking at me, and I was so embarrassed. What was there to say? Well, I'm not going to lie. This hurt. I already felt bad for being fat, ugly, a college drop-out, and pretty much a failure. I already felt bad about being scared of girls and shy, and not the smooth and comfortable person that so many guys seemed to be. I was the awkward guy. Not even the funny fat guy, but just the depressed fat guy.

I had to face my friends and tell them what happened. But after that I didn't ask many girls to dance. There were some girls who were just my friends, and we would dance.

After eventually regaining the nerve to ask girls to dance, I never asked another "eye candy" girl. I wasn't in that league and never would be.

What about blind dates? People set those up often, but most of them were absolute disasters! One of my first blind dates was with Lisa, the twin sister of my friend's girlfriend. It was great that he wanted to set me up and I agreed to go. These twins were still in high school and they wanted us to go to the dance as two couples. Neither girl was considered popular at all, so this setup was the only way they'd be going. I was happy to be the guy that took Lisa to the dance, but my self-esteem was at an all-time low.

When we arrived at their house and picked up the girls, Lisa was immediately standoffish and not friendly at all, but I figured she was just nervous.

We drove to a grocery store, walking around collecting items for a picnic. In the store, my friend, his girlfriend and I all walked together, while Lisa hung back about 20 feet. This was kind of odd—she wouldn't even walk with us! So I asked her what was up, and she answered, *"Nothing."* She explained she just wasn't comfortable being in our group.

It was clear that accepting this blind date was a mistake, and the night only continued to get worse. Lisa was actually becoming more and more standoffish and even rude. She plainly didn't want to be with me. Well, OK. She was disappointed in me as her date. Well, OK then.

"Lisa, do you want to go home?" I asked.

"No. I want to go to the dance," she answered.

So we went to the dance and took very uncomfortable group pictures, and then Lisa disappeared entirely. I sat on the side of the room and just watched all the others dance. Lisa's sister apologized profusely for Lisa ditching me. Word spread through the entire dance that she had ditched me, and a few other girls asked me to dance just to cheer me up. I don't know where Lisa went or what happened, but I ended up leaving early and going home. This was devastating! I was taking a girl who was not going to get asked to go to her own dance. I paid for everything, got all the doors, and had driven us all there. I wasn't even in high school anymore but I went with her, and then it ended the way it did. Nothing about this was comfortable. Why couldn't I make her happy?

A few weeks later my friend called, asking if I was OK.

"Sure," I told him, "I'm over it."

He said that Lisa wasn't comfortable in that setting and had gone home nervous, and that she really wanted to make it up to me. Well, as a very forgiving person and maybe saying *yes* more than I should, I agreed to go with them on another group date and give Lisa another chance.

We all decided to go roller skating. There was a roller rink in our town and it was pretty popular. Skating wasn't my best sport but it was really fun to go, so we grabbed some food at a Chinese place on the way and then headed to the skate center.

Things were fairly OK in the beginning. Lisa was not as standoffish, but was still not talkative or overly friendly. When we got to the rink, we all began skating around like you normally do. This was supposed to be a double date, but Lisa was skating quite a bit ahead of our group. At least my friend and Lisa's sister skated and talked with me.

The announcer at the rink would frequently call out different skating styles every few songs. Sometimes it would be all guys skating, all girls skating, a reverse direction song, or a song where you had to skate backwards the whole time. Then once in a while it was a couples skating song, where you joined hands and skated around the rink together. Usually we'd sit this one out, but on this occasion I asked Lisa. That is, I asked her, and she very quickly said, "No thanks, I don't feel like it."

So, we sat on the sidelines and watched the carefree skaters. Lisa excused herself to go to the restroom and walked away. After a little bit her sister and my friend came over and sat down. They asked where Lisa was. "I think she went to the bathroom but I'm not sure," I answered.

And then we all saw it. Not one of us moved or said a word as Lisa went skating by us in the crowded rink, holding another guy's hand! My friend said some choice words that I will not repeat in this book, but he was very, very angry with Lisa. Her sister was really embarrassed and once again began to apologize for Lisa's behavior. She probably had to do that a lot.

As for me, I was just blown away and actually shocked. She burned me again! She ditched me—again. I took her out twice, paid both times, and she ditched me. This time, being very mad, I stood up and announced, "I'm leaving!"

It didn't matter what the others did, but my friend and Lisa's sister came with me, and we left Lisa at the roller rink without telling her a thing. The rink was a good 45 minutes away from her house, and we just walked out and drove away. I dropped off the other two as they apologized once again. After that, I never saw Lisa or talked to her again, and rarely saw my friend and his girlfriend.

Something in me snapped that night. I'd never be that pushover, vulnerable guy again. A "Lisa" would never again burn me one time, let alone two! This was the beginning of a few rocky years of dating. Being really down in the dumps, and trying to get away from it, I started taking an interest in horses. Horses were an outlet for my stress, and I was making some good friends as I learned more and more about these wonderful animals.

Much of my life was then spent surrounded by horses. This consumed most of my free time, and there was little pressure to date due to being so busy. Something about working with and learning from the horse made me feel more complete, and not a total failure. However, I was still feeling depressed and gaining weight.

My community was very focused on religion, and most kids my age were going on religious missions. The girls in this age group were raised to look for these guys. I have always been very spiritual, but at many times in my life not very religious. So, just like dropping out of college, I was also not fitting the mold that my community had for people my age. This caused many girls to not want to go out with me. One girl I asked out literally said, "I will not go out with you because you are not going on a church mission." I felt very judged and very hurt by the reactions of the girls my age.

Some girls' dads even told me that since I was not going on a religious mission, their daughters were not *allowed* to go out with me. Well, you do have to admire their honesty, but this caused me to become even angrier, and I stopped going to church altogether.

And why didn't I go on a mission? My depression problems, fear and anxiety kept me from it, but at the same time I felt like it was nobody's business what was going on with me.

There were a few blind dates during that time, but they resulted in odd or uncomfortable experiences. I remember going on one group blind date and picking the girl up. My style was country music, horses, camping, and the whole country life. I had cowboy boots and hats, but I wasn't dressed like that when I picked up my date.

As we headed to my truck, small talk seemed like a good idea, so I asked a familiar question: "What kind of music do you like?"

"Oh, I like all music except for that cowboy country garbage.

Anything but that!"

"Oh, yeah." I laughed a little, and realized this could be a very long date. With this group of people we were going to make tinfoil dinners and watch a movie at my house.

At home, I got the fire going out back, got all the dinners wrapped, and started cooking the meals. But it was just me, out there all alone. The rest of the group stayed in the house laughing and talking.

Sitting next to the fire by myself, cooking the dinners, I wondered why it meant so much to me, when nobody else in this group seemed to care. How could I get set up with a person or group of people who were so wrong for me? Did you have to let go of what you love to find someone? Was my life really that different from the normal?

The dinners were safely cooking so I went into the house and asked my date if she might want to come out and sit by the fire with me.

"NO, I don't want to smell like campfire! I hate that smell."

Well, I love the crackle of a campfire, the smell of burning fire wood, and being under the star-filled sky. This date was over before it started and there was no point in wasting any more time. After dinner I declared the night finished and took everyone home. I don't remember my date's name or anything about her, only how bad the night was.

Another time I asked a girl in my neighborhood to a Toby Keith concert. I had tickets and wanted to take someone new. I got up the nerve to ask her, and she stood there and stared blankly at me, asking, "Who is Toby Keith?"

While I explained who he was she just interrupted and said bluntly, "You know what? No thanks. I don't really want to go."

It hurt, yes, but I was getting used to this, or maybe just becoming numb to rejection. At this point, going through the motions of trying to date, in a way I was that bullied kid all over again. But still I was determined to find someone!

There was another girl I knew of—surely she would go to this concert. The very same night of my last rejection I asked her, and got a yes! Great—off to a good start then.

The following weekend I headed over to pick her up and knocked on the door.

"Come on in!" she yelled from inside.

As I opened the door there she was, sitting on her couch with two other guys. One had his arms around her, snuggled up close. Talk about uncomfortable! But she just said, "Oh yeah, the concert. OK guys, I'll be back in a few hours."

Then she stood up and walked out with me, leaving the other two guys on the couch. What was that all about?

And what was behind so many strange and bad situations with girls? They either won't date me because I'm fat, or not a missionary, or the ones who will go out with me are just using me. What was I doing wrong? There was no sense in any of this.

Dating? I was about done with it. My friends were all finding people and getting girlfriends, but I wasn't doing so well. The situation was getting desperate. Despite trying numerous blind dates, most were very uncomfortable and awkward, and I couldn't wait for them to end. There were even dates where I got confronted by ex-boyfriends and threatened for going out with "their girlfriends." I even tried going back to church and meeting some of those girls.

There was a singles program in our area. Singles of a certain age would all go to church together and have weekly activities and dances. Why not try this group? Thankfully, my life began to improve. I had found a good place. There were lots of people my age, and all single. It was easy to make friends and go to activities. There wasn't much dating anymore but I enjoyed going to lots of group activities.

The first blind date where I actually had fun was with a girl named Valerie. Val and I would end up becoming great friends for years to come. As far as a relationship went it didn't end up being right, but we loved to spend time together. Valerie restored my faith in women as I finally knew what a good date was and a good human being. As the years went on I got invited to be part of dating groups, speed dating, and many other social dating activities. I even signed up for half a dozen online dating sites. Yes, there really are that many and a whole lot more.

Surely the more sites I used, the better chance of finding the perfect girl for me. Well, after meeting the first "online girl" for a date, and finding out she looked nothing like her profile and was nothing like she described, I went home and deleted all my profiles. Never again have I been back online. No—not going to set myself up to be burned like in years past.

Well, as years went by, I met Emma at a potluck for singles our age, and we were friends instantly. Emma was amazing! She was tall, beautiful, fun, drove a sports car, had a house, pushed me out of my comfort zone on many occasions, and made me laugh. Emma was pretty much everything anyone should have wanted. And we did date, we did have a connection and spent a lot of time together. We were very comfortable and spent years being best friends. However, the closer she got, the more I would push her away.

Once we were out to lunch together, having a great time, laughing and being our goofy selves as usual. She didn't care what others thought of her and I always wanted that for myself, because I cared way too much! At the restaurant, we ran into a couple of my acquaintances so we walked over to their table and I introduced them to Emma. Then a waitress came over and started talking to us all. This waitress had waited on me many times and was flirtatious, attractive, and a solid waitress to boot. She flirted with the older guys we were talking to, making them feel special like good waitresses do.

After a brief chat, Emma and I left the restaurant and I headed back to my day job, working with Dad at an electrical supply company.

Thirty minutes later, these same two guys from lunch stopped by the office to talk to me. One of them was very serious and he said, "Eric, what are you doing? Why are you wasting your time with that girl you were with? Please tell me you're just friends. We want you to go out with the waitress that was helping us. She seemed more your type."

What? They also said some not-so-nice things that they really didn't know anything about! How did they possibly know "my type" when I didn't even know? This was my friend they were talking about, and these words hurt. Unfortunately, since I cared too much about what others thought, their words began to cause doubt.

Was the relationship with Emma a mistake? What was I not seeing? This strange doubt that crept into my mind ultimately destroyed what Emma and I had. I lost out on something amazing—all based on comments from people whose thoughts should have meant nothing to me!

And guess what? Neither of those guys had a relationship worth bragging about, so why were they lecturing me?

Those guys were wrong all the way, but listening to them would prove to be a pivotal moment in my life, because my fears were getting the best of me. How did these fears get so ingrained? I don't know—but they were bad. These fears prevented anyone from getting close enough to hurt me. The relationship with Emma was perfect, and I had actually just walked away and there was no way to ever get back what we had!

As time passed, doubting myself over and over again became a habit. It happened too many times in the years to come. Since being deeply hurt when I was younger and trying to date, it seemed the past had successfully built a wall to protect me, even though I was now older. Maybe it was a built-in protection mechanism, or maybe it was a fear of losing someone. Maybe it was a fear of failing. Was it something bigger than me?

We have so many fears when it comes to dating and relationships, and as for me, I was just not ready to face them. Where was the strength to face those fears? It was true that I got stomped on years ago, but now something was keeping me from experiencing the life of my desires and blocking happiness.

On the outside I had changed a whole lot, finally losing the weight I'd picked up before, but that overweight bullied kid? It seemed he was still stuck on the inside. Fixing this would prove to be quite the challenge.

There are countless stories of blind dates, dating, and failed and uncomfortable dates not mentioned. There could be some girls that dated me in my past who might read this book and get offended. If this is offensive, I'm very sorry, but it's the truth. In my dating life I have been stood up, rejected, made fun of, used, tricked, and whatever else could possibly happen when you date. I could probably write a whole book on my dating life. But at least I really tried, right?

Some people have asked me over the years how these experiences have not made me into a bitter and angry person. It would be a lie to say that it hasn't affected me, but it has not made me angry. These experiences have caused me to be guarded in many types of situations, but this has been an instrumental part of my journey and I would not trade it for anything. My many experiences in the past have brought me to the path that I'm on today.

9 HORSES

"When I hear somebody talk about a horse or cow being stupid,
I figure it's a sure sign that the animal has somehow outfoxed them."
—Tom Dorrance, *True Unity: Willing Communication
Between Horse & Human*

While all of that was going on with the dating issues there was something else happening in my life. I've mentioned my horses. As my love and thirst for knowing more about the horse grew, so did I. My health, mentally and physically, as well as my self-esteem and courage all improved. Horses would prove to be a big part of my life and in fact, horses would save my life.

So, because I had been rejected in the dating world so much, I decided to devote myself to horses. Having developed social anxiety, there was no interest in being part of anything that had a crowd. I just wanted to work, pay the bills, and get a horse. So began my horse phase.

Many of us probably want a horse growing up, and I sure did. My grandpa was a real cowboy, and I wanted to be one too, but my parents said, "Son, you've got to wait until you're old enough to purchase your own."

When Grandpa Dodge suffered some serious health setbacks he had to sell his cows and horses, and the family ranch was leased to another rancher, so that part of my life had sort of faded away. But now it was up to me to bring it back. I would follow in my grandfather's footsteps and start riding horses again!

At the time, my mother had a friend named Ann who was also getting into horses, and she told me to go ride her horse a few times to make sure I really wanted to do this. Ann's horse was named Bo. Bo was fun to ride, and I'd go see him any time I had the chance.

Riding lessons came first as I started to learn everything possible about horses. The methods they used seemed quite traditional and somewhat harsh at times, but I didn't know any better. Since my grandpa was a cowboy and a horseman, I could definitely be one, and on impulse bought a horse of my very own.

I went for the first horse I saw that was big, pretty, and classified as a kid's horse by the guy selling it. But this was a horrible mistake, because this mare had all kinds of problems and actually became very dangerous. Ginger sure knew how to take advantage of me, an inexperienced horseman. Many times, while trying to get a bit in her mouth or load her in a trailer, she'd lose her temper and explode!

Ginger could end up hurting or even killing me, so I hired the people giving me riding lessons to work with my horse and see if they could make something good out of her. I watched them tie Ginger to an arena post and try to get her to take a bit by drenching it with honey and oats. When she pulled back from the bit, they would whip her on the head with a stock whip and tie a squeeze rope around her stomach to cut off her air supply if she pulled back. The harder she pulled, the more it hurt her. This horse was so persistent and strong-willed. Looking back, I respect her for this. I saw Ginger tear the whole side of the arena off and walk back to her stall in defiance.

In the few weeks since I'd bought her, Ginger was starting to look skinny and her ribs were showing. Her stomach looked very distended and we thought she had worms. We wormed her of course, and the facility trainers said she had hay belly and that we needed to ride her a whole lot more and work it off by doing more cardio.

Going out to ride the next day I found the trainer lying in the tack shed, knocked unconscious and bleeding. When she came to she was very disoriented, and couldn't remember what had happened. She didn't recall if she'd been working my horse or another horse when she got nailed. Even though she said she didn't think it was Ginger, this incident was really scary.

I sure loved horses, but had a lot of anxiety about my horse at the time, developing a huge fear around horses generally. No, this could not happen—but it did. The fear got so bad I was ready to sell Ginger and quit riding altogether.

Then I met Don, an amazing trainer in my town. I had heard all about him from other people in the horse industry. I decided to give him a call. Don was a natural horseman and believed in gentle training techniques. He introduced me to legendary trainers like Tom Dorrance,

Ray Hunt, Buck Brannaman, and many more. This subject alone could be another whole book but, once again, that's not why we are here.

Now, nobody could get Ginger into a trailer without the atom bomb inside her going off. On the phone, this new trainer told me, "How about this? If I can get your horse in a trailer, will you let me work with you?"

I said, "What do you mean, Don, work with *me*? The horse has tons of problems."

"No," he said. "The human has the problems, the horse knows what she is doing."

Well, I thought this guy Don was a quack. After what I'd seen I didn't believe anyone could get my horse in a trailer or get her to cooperate in any way.

"Yeah Don," I almost laughed, "you've got a deal."

Well, Don showed up less than an hour later and within 20 minutes, Ginger was calmly standing in the trailer. That was incredible! I left the original trainers and never looked back.

Don completely changed my outlook on life in general. He spent a lot of time reprogramming me to look at things differently with the horse.

First off, I told him my horse couldn't take a bit.

He simply said, "You want to bet?" And then he proved me wrong.

I also told him my horse needed tie downs, or she'd throw her head and rear.

"You wanna bet?" Don said once more, and he proved me wrong yet again. His proving me wrong became a habit!

Don could get horses to do anything because he was so good at understanding them. I worked with him for eight years while accumulating 12 horses and several head of cows. I even began making Don's business cards and helped him set up clinics, kind of becoming his marketing department. After all, I was still working at the company my dad was managing, and had worked my way up into a desk job in sales and marketing.

It seemed I was a natural at sales and marketing, but I just wanted to be better at horses, and I learned so much about *life* from horses and Don. Oh, and by the way, two weeks after moving my horse to Don's, remember the hay belly we needed to work on? Well, it turned out to be a baby filly we named Nutmeg. Seems appropriate since her mama was named Ginger. We had not even known that Ginger was pregnant!

Having now had several horses, each has been connected with me in many different ways. There was a wild horse that my friend Kade and I found living out in the sagebrush foothills of the mountains close to our family ranch. She was a beautiful dapple gray, almost purple-colored Quarter Horse mare. She was thick and muscular and had a very long silver mane and tail that would flow as she would run. We named her Smokey, and spent a few summers trying to feed and catch her. We'd lie down in the sagebrush and hold carrots up for Smokey to eat, trying to be as non-threatening as possible. We never could get close enough to pet Smokey, but we had a whole lot of fun with this horse. A few years later she disappeared on us. I like to think that Smokey moved on to greener pastures or found a herd that she could belong to.

Over the years I've also had a few different racehorses that were rescued from the track. There was Neverlee who had a chipped knee, but she was a really sweet horse, and she brought us another baby named Streaklee. Luna was adopted one weekend in Arizona while I was working at a horse clinic with Don. Luna was a very large and quiet horse, and me being a tall and large person, I felt comfortable on a large horse. However, Luna proved to be very clumsy on the trails, and nearly fell down with me on multiple occasions. He was also too big for my trailer, and so every time he got in he'd hit his head on the roof and cut himself, causing him to panic and throw a fit. After that I stopped feeling safe with him.

There was Nutmeg, Bubba, Buddy, Jessie, Ginger #2, and one of my favorites was Tubby. Tubby was a very old horse that his owners had neglected. They offered him to me for a steal of a deal.

A friend of the owners had given this horse to them, and they'd never ridden him or anything. They didn't know how old he was, what kind of horse he was, or even if Tubby was a he or a she. So off I went to see Tubby. He was really ragged and beat-up. He was also severely overweight, and that's why I called him Tubby. Evidently the owners would toss a full bale of hay into his corral and leave, figuring he could eat off the bale for almost a week before they had to come back and check on him.

Tubby's hair was knotted up and his hooves were curling up. They had not been trimmed in a long time. His eyes were runny and he looked kind of lifeless. Nobody had brushed him in many months.

But something in his eye was very calming and reassuring. We connected the second I set foot in his corral, and I knew he was going to be my horse. With any other horse I'd never have done this, but Tubby just had a feel about him, so with an old halter that was hanging on the fence I walked him around a little. Within about five minutes I fully trusted this horse, and that had never happened before, especially with a horse that was unknown! Normally the process would take time to ensure the horse would not run away or buck me off, but Tubby was different. So with nothing but the halter and lead rope, I jumped on him bareback and off we went.

Tubby had been very lonely in that coral of his and he was definitely relieved to see me. So I brushed him and rode him. He felt like he was given a purpose again. And I did something else that even today just would not happen—I opened the gate and rode away from the corral. This must have been quite the sight. Here was a 6'4" overweight kid riding down the road bareback on a short, stubby, mangy old horse with no bridal or bit, having the time of our lives. Tubby was solid and trustworthy.

As we made our way slowly down the road, suddenly a flock of giant ostriches broke free from their pen and started running towards us! Most horses would panic over seeing something like this. Most would spin dramatically and head for the hills, so I braced myself, fully expecting this herd of massive, long-legged birds to end my peaceful ride on Tubby. Something else happened though. Tubby put his ears back and headed right for the menacing flock! Ostriches can do terrible damage with their feet, but they cleared a path for us and we were not hurt in the least.

Tubby was one tough old horse who didn't have an ounce of spook in him. He was safe. I trusted him and he trusted me. Tubby was now my horse, so I bought him and home we went.

Tubby and I had a wonderful summer. He was and still is my favorite horse of all times. Sadly, he ended up getting bad arthritis in his legs within the year and could no longer carry me. His legs were weak and he would trip and sometimes fall when I was riding him. My weight was just too much for him and I couldn't afford to keep him as a pet only.

I did some searching and found Tubby a good retirement home with a kind owner who was a lot smaller than me and didn't ride him very much. In fact, it ended up being a small, lightweight, 7-year-old girl who absolutely loved him to death! The family promised to give him a good home for the rest of his life. I was sad to see him go but very happy to see him go to this wonderful home.

Never will I forget the day I met that horse. No horse since has been a Tubby. While I've had some really good and fun horses, there were none that I'd trust with my life like I did that horse. I'll always be looking for another Tubby.

To this day, I still have horses and still talk to Don. I still study the ways of the natural horsemen and the horse whisperers. I have met many other trainers, horsemen and horsewomen that I respect and love learning from. And we can learn a lot about life itself through our animals as well.

You are probably asking yourself why is Eric writing all this stuff about horses? Well, when I was down and depressed and had nowhere to turn, I had my horses. When I focused my energy on something I loved, my life and my health would improve. When I didn't feel like leaving the house or doing anything at all, I would just need to go walk my dog or feed my horses or pet Bart, my cat. My animals were always there for me. The horses taught me that just because you see something, and you are sure of something, it doesn't mean that it is right. If it isn't working the way you are doing it, don't give up, just change things a little.

Importantly, I learned patience—that gentle persuasion works better than forceful persuasion. And best of all, I didn't quit horses.

When things in life seem impossible, step back and look at the situation in a different way. When it came to the horse, **everything I thought was impossible ended up being very possible**. I cannot emphasize this enough! In fact, not only was it *not impossible*, it was very easy.

I have now had 10 horses in my life. Each and every horse has taught me something about myself. All of my animals have, really, and my dogs and cats are just as important to me as my horses. My animals saved my life. Horses gave me an outlet and gave me something to be part of. I will always cherish my horse days and will always be a better person because of what my horses have taught me.

What do you love to do? Do you have activities that give you an escape from your normal everyday life? I recommend that you make a list and try to find what you really love to do, or search for hobbies. Think about volunteering with children, animals, or people who need help in one way or another. This truly was a huge step for me in finding happiness.

My dad riding Tubby at our family ranch.
Nutmeg is following behind.

My dad taking my sister and I on our first horse ride. This is my
grandpa's horse, Star Fire.

My nephews riding Jessie.

10 GETTING HEALTHY

"Let food be thy medicine and medicine be thy food."
—Hippocrates

Remember Valerie? She was the very avid hiker and outdoors-woman who restored my faith in dating. Valerie and I really had fun but I knew I was out of shape, overweight, and could not keep up. My horse was also having a hard time packing my heavy behind up into the backcountry. So I decided it was time to get myself in shape! To start off, I took some awesome pills that were supposed to make you lose weight, and fast. Amazingly, after taking them, I simply wasn't hungry anymore.

Wow—I lost 30 pounds in 30 days on these miracle pills! Many people thought I was sick because the weight melted off so fast, but what did they know? I started exercising and began to hike with Valerie. And now carrying a lot less weight and surely healthy, I'd go get life insurance.

The life insurance application required a physical. No problem! Off I went for some blood tests and answered a bunch of questions. And a couple of days later, the phone rang.

"Hello, this is Eric," I said.

"Mr. Dodge, this is Derek Smith and I'm calling about your health screening."

"That was quick—this is pretty good customer service."

"Mr. Dodge, listen to me: your liver is failing. You need to get to the hospital ASAP!"

"What? Are you kidding?" This insurance guy had to be joking with me!

"I truly wish I was kidding, Mr. Dodge, but this is serious. You've got to get to a hospital now!"

My liver? There's only one of those, right? A cold chill ran over me and I was in utter terror about my future at this point. I got to the doctor as fast as I could get an appointment. They ran many tests: checked my liver, my bones, my intestines, and anything else that could cause my liver enzymes to be that far out of line. But they could find nothing wrong with me! Was I dying or not?

To this day, I still have problems, and we can't find out what causes them. I do often wonder if it wasn't because of those weight loss pills. Only after the doctors gave me the all-clear, backed by all the notes and tests, was I able to get the life insurance.

I had really thought I was dying! So after that big scare I decided to treat life differently. The thing to do was to really get healthy, get in shape, and take better care of myself. With this goal in mind I joined a local weight loss center to learn about nutrition and exercise. Another 30 pounds was burned off with their help, and this was my lowest weight in years. I started riding my mountain bike, hiking with Val and some of my other friends, and started to enjoy life to the fullest once again.

Here's more of my weight loss story in full detail. I'm going to give you personal details so it really makes sense.

When I graduated high school I was 6' 2" and weighed 223 pounds. To begin, I joined a gym and hired a personal trainer. They started to build muscle but didn't do much for cardio. Despite the training, I started to eat more and got lazier as time went on, and I was dealing more and more with depression and anxiety. So even though I was going to the gym a little bit, the weight was packing on steadily. Within a few years I was 265 pounds and 6' 4" tall. Despite my greater height, the weight made me insecure and depressed. I totally understand the cycle of not having any energy to lose weight, yet knowing that if I could just lose a few pounds, I would get the energy to continue losing weight! At this point, nothing helped.

It was tough to find clothes that fit. Plus I didn't feel good physically, and was downright embarrassed about my appearance. This is when I discovered that "miracle" product I mentioned earlier. It was a pill filled with ephedra. Ephedra is the stuff outlawed by the Food and Drug Administration for causing health problems.

To get results, I started taking the maximum dose and oh, did it work! I had energy, I wasn't hungry, and like I said, lost 30 pounds in 30 days. I was almost back to my high school weight of 223 pounds and being 2 inches taller, this was good news. Once ephedra was outlawed I stopped taking that pill and guess what? Yep, the weight came back.

Being very upset I immediately tried Slim Fast, but that didn't work well for me at all. That's OK, there were other options, as I jumped to Atkins, South Beach, LA Weight Loss, Nutrisystem, you name it. None of these were working! Sure, I lost weight with them all but it always just came back—they just weren't sustainable for me long term.

Finally I joined a different weight loss center in my town, and had weight loss coaches helping me for several hundred dollars. Getting weighed in front of these ladies every week and having to talk about my eating really helped me, and the weight started to come off again. The scale told the story as I slowly passed my goal of 223 lbs. once more, and went all the way down to 205.

This was amazing, and people were blown away! I'd never been at this weight. However, this program had supplements and ways of eating, so as soon as I graduated and left the program, it started to come back! I got on the scale after a while and was right back to 230 again. This was devastating, so I went and joined the weight loss center once more and what do you know, I again lost the weight. Within three months the scale was back to 205 pounds. I stayed with these folks, but eventually that weight loss center went out of business.

While looking for a new weight loss place I started hiking more, bought a mountain bike, went to the gym, and so on, but nothing seemed to help me lose the weight like the food and eating programs did. If I wasn't on some sort of a diet then the weight came right back, even with exercise. So what did I do? Certainly this was possible all on my own without paying for a weight loss center! But even with my working out I failed to realize I was eating poorly again.

One day it was brought to my attention that I was not skinny anymore. That person was very rude, but today I really thank him. The scale showed my weight back to almost 250 pounds. Depressing? Yes!

Then my brother Andy told me, "I am going to *make you* lose weight!"

Andy took me to a clinic where a doctor prescribed some weight loss meds and signed me up for a new diet called HCG. This diet was sheer hell and I hated it! I was weak, sore, and almost passed out daily. I was actually mean to everyone because I was starving! Even with doctor supervision, and taking all kinds of other meds to offset the side effects of starving, there was nothing to like about it.

Well, I did lose weight—35 pounds in 25 days to be exact. It was so fast yet so horrible. I went onto their maintenance plan and then eventually went off it. And guess what? Within two weeks I'd gained back half of what I lost! This was terrible and I didn't know what to do.

Everyone kept saying *you need to join Weight Watchers*. Well, I'd heard so much about Weight Watchers, but to me it was just a program for a bunch of ladies to get together and talk about weight loss. It wasn't a program for men. Then one day I saw a guy logged into a cool program on the computer. It said "Weight Watchers Online" and that caught my interest. This guy told me all about it, and about his own weight loss. It actually said on the screen, Weight Watchers for Men. OK, I was totally on board and signed up that very day.

It was so easy. I didn't have to do some crazy cleanse for two days followed by two awful days of fasting, and so on. I didn't have to drink some fancy juice for two weeks like on the Hollywood diet. I didn't have to (LOAD) or (Starve) like on other diets. I just posted my weight and it told me what food values were, and off I went, tracking my meals and keeping everything under my recommended values number.

So, let me tell you what has happened. I've been a member of Weight Watchers for Men for many years now. I've lost all my weight and *not gained it back!* Whenever a few pounds creep on, I just start tracking what foods I eat. The program begins to make me accountable again and the weight starts to come off. Since I signed up many of my friends and family have signed up as well. All of them have lost large amounts of weight.

I eat out every day of my life, and everyone knows how much diet soda I drink. Certainly I've had to make some changes, but I don't ever go hungry. If there's a bad week when I travel, I can just go right back on the plan and get back to my weight. I don't care if I never try another diet or eating program again, because I'm content where I am. As a current lifetime member, I hope to be one always. I'm never hungry, and still after all these years that weight has stayed off! Currently I'm about 185 pounds and it is stable. I still go to meetings and love to learn about health and fitness.

I am not sponsored or endorsed by Weight Watchers; I am just forever grateful for what they've done for my family and myself. They saved my life as well as my mom's and dad's lives. My mom is down 130 pounds and has reversed her diabetes, sleep apnea, oxygen use, and even done some half marathons in her 50's and 60's. Health is so important for our happiness and self-esteem.

I'm an advocate for health. I would say the pursuit of better health is the single most important thing I've done to feel better and find happiness.

Every year I set a health goal. Whether it's to drink more water, walk more steps, lose more weight, or list certain hikes to achieve, I always have a health goal. Healthy is happy. Even just going for a simple walk around the block when you feel a little blue will begin to release endorphins into your brain, instantly lifting your mood. Maybe it's something simple like pulling weeds or planting flowers, or just sitting in the sun and reading a book. I can't say enough about this. For instance, I always mow my own yard and clean it up weekly. I've tried to hire it out, and certainly as much as I travel that could be justified. However, when I get finished mowing, trimming, watering, and exercising as I work my yard into tip-top shape, I just feel much better all over. It has nothing to do with saving the money every week and has everything to do with being happier.

Try it. Just do some small things outside this week and watch your mood increase. I've begun to love riding my bike down by the river, swimming at our rec center, walking my dog out in the hills, and geocaching. Geocaching is using a cell phone app or satellite GPS to search for fun little hidden treasures. It keeps me active, challenges me, and is just a fun way to get movement in. I challenge you to do the same. Park your car in the farthest stall from the store, anything like that. Just start moving more and you will be happier.

Before and After photo.

11 HOW I BECAME A SINGER

"A ship is safe in harbor, but that's not what ships are for."
—William G.T. Shedd

You read the chapter on the loss of Grandpa Elmer, my mom's dad, so you know how hard that was. Now imagine what would happen when another even closer grandparent was ailing.

It was August of 2001 and my cowboy grandpa, my Grandpa Dodge, was dying. This man was very close to me. With our common love of horses and cattle, I was not ready for him to go. How could I possibly make it through that?

I had just built my home out in the fields where we used to have our family Easter picnics. One midnight I'd just gotten into bed when my mother called me.

"Hello Mom," I said, wondering why she was calling so late.

"Eric, Grandpa has passed away. We're outside right now."

My family knew I'd take it hard and they were at my house in case I needed them. Because I was very tired it just did not fully sink in.

"It's OK," I told them. "You all can go back home."

I went back to bed and actually slept, but the next day I was in shock. Yes, we'd all known it was coming but I couldn't have fully prepared for the wave of sadness.

At the funeral my grandmother wanted all the cousins to sing a song to honor my grandfather. She chose the popular hymn, "How Great Thou Art." Because of my huge fear of being in front of crowds, there was no way I was singing. In person and on the phone, I simply told the family it wasn't going to happen. Even though there were like ten people in the group, my gut told me I was not capable.

This really hurt my mother and grandmother, but I just couldn't do it—couldn't sing, couldn't stand on that platform. I might not be able to handle even going to the funeral! I put my foot down and flat out said **no**.

This upset my mom to no end, and she said, "Well, I hope you sing at *my* funeral."

My mom knew I could sing, and she told me that often. She'd hear me whistling songs around the house, and I'd add vibrato to my whistling. Mom said, "If you can whistle like that, Eric, you can sing."

After much pressure and many pep talks from my family, I reconsidered singing with my cousins. Well, at least I stood on the platform with them. I did not actually sing a note, but held the songbook, mouthed the words and pretended.

The funeral went as well as funerals can go. I certainly don't like them and surely never will. I was however proud of myself for accomplishing two very difficult things: going to a funeral, and standing on a stage and singing—sort of.

Even though my mother thought so, I really didn't know if I could sing very well. Sure, I'd sing in my car, but only when people weren't around. I sounded all right I guess, but decided that everyone thinks they sound all right to themselves.

A few friends would still go out to the country dance place, and I decided to go out there to take my mind off things. That night the DJ dared my friend Dave to sing a song. Well, Dave jumped right up without a second thought and sang his heart out! It happened to be one of my favorites, "Keeper Of The Stars" by Tracy Byrd. Dave did pretty well, and I was blown away. I never knew he could sing a note, and yet he was willing to take a chance and jump up there just for fun. Over the weeks to come I thought about that often.

And this is where the story takes a turn. I'd decided to become a police officer or a wildlife conservation officer. Even as a little kid, it was something that interested me—police officer, fire fighter, veterinarian; you name it. I had a friend on the local force and she brought me all the books, and got me in touch with the right people to get all the physical test requirements. I started working towards taking this test during the month of August 2001.

Also, in the meantime and on a whim I entered my name in a drawing from our local radio station. It was a chance at winning a free cruise. Everyone who entered had to be listening to 98.1 FM at a certain time, and if they drew your name, you had 9 minutes and 8 seconds to call in.

The day of the drawing I was working with Dad and running a delivery to a customer. The truck radio was tuned to 98.1, and as I was driving the DJ called out the name of a relative of mine, strangely enough!

Darlene? There was no way Darlene *would not* call in, so I just got out of the truck and dropped off the delivery, because that contest was now over.

After speaking with our customer and getting back in the truck to leave, the DJ was counting down the last 10 seconds. *Darlene had not called in.* Wow—there was another chance at this!

Then somehow, I just knew they were going to call my name. I could actually feel it. *They are gonna call my name.*

The sound of papers rustling around in the hat crackled over the air as they got ready to draw. Bob, the DJ, pulled the paper out and announced, "Our next name is ERIC DODGE."

My mouth fell open and my eyes went wide. Oh my gosh—how did I know it was going to be me? I was literally stunned.

I'd never won anything before and had never really traveled much, but I had just won an all-expenses paid cruise with airfare. Amazing! I grabbed my cell phone and dialed in within 10 seconds, even though it felt like it took a lifetime. But wait—how was I going to talk to a DJ over the radio heard by thousands of people without freezing up?

I made it past the call screener with sweat pouring out of me. My heart was pounding like it wanted out of my chest and out of the truck as well. And next I was about to be live on air with DJ Bob!

"So Eric," Bob asked, "Who are you going to take?"

"Oh, I'll probably take my brother Ashton with me," I replied.

You could hear my voice shaking just a little from the fear of being on the radio but I didn't care. I was way too excited at this point.

"Well Eric, if Ashton can't go," Bob laughed, "I have a couple of daughters that would love to go!"

Whew, I made it through the on-air chat and hadn't passed out or lost it. And later in life, by chance, I'd come to be great friends with DJ Bob, his daughters, and his whole family.

Well, the cruise was set! Ashton and I had to go sooner than expected as they wanted us to pick a time in just the next few weeks. We picked Sept 10th, 2001 to depart from Los Angeles, California to Mexico. I was nervous but excited to get away. Something like this trip might help me get over the loss of my grandfather.

The night of September 10th we set sail and headed into Mexico. We were on an older and smaller cruise ship than the rest of the fleet, but to me it was very nice. It had several floors and in my eyes it was a massive floating city. There was tons of food and we ate all night long as we walked through each and every attraction on the ship. They had a casino, a comedy club, an arcade, a dance floor, a shopping mall, and much more. This was something we had never experienced before.

Well, the next morning was September 11th, 2001. We awoke to the television showing all kinds of unbelievable, horrible things happening back home! We were in shock! Was this war?

We'd also paid for an offshore excursion in Ensenada, Mexico and the attacks on our country back home were still unfolding as we left on the bus. We saw heavily armed troops all over, and on the bus our tour guide was crying as she told us what was happening back home.

In Mexico the reports were very inaccurate. They were telling us that L.A. was also being attacked and that we didn't have a port to return to. The next news was that cruise ships might also be attacked. Our excursion was cut short as the government of Mexico ordered us all aboard the ship, and to get our cruise ship out of their harbor!

You remember where you were that day, don't you? For all of us, whether at home or outside the U.S., it was nerve-racking.

As we all streamed back onboard, the captain announced that the ship's phones would be free for an hour so we could call our families. Then they announced that the U.S. Coast Guard was flying in with helicopters, and we would all need to leave our rooms while they searched them with bomb-sniffing dogs.

Ashton and I were both stressed out but did as they told us. Somehow we ended up at the karaoke lounge on the top deck. We were sitting there, looking down at the beautiful blue sea and talking about life, when Ashton said, "Isn't it weird that we may never make it home? Makes you think you should do everything you want to do before it's too late. What have you wanted to do, Eric?"

"Ashton, I've always wanted to try singing a solo but have been way too scared." I looked over at Ashton, then down at the floor. There was nothing else to say.

A bunch of jumbled thoughts started up in my mind and I didn't notice Ashton anymore, but within minutes, I heard my name being called.

Eric—as in me? The karaoke DJ was calling me up to come sing a song! *What?* I was in shock. Ashton had entered my name. What was I going to do now?

When your life is flashing before your eyes, you begin to think differently. With the unimaginable attacks going on at home, it was possible that this chance would never come again. With that thought running through my mind, I stood up.

The song I picked was "The Dance" by Garth Brooks. With the microphone in my hand, I stared only at the screen and the floor the whole time—and sang my heart out. I sang the whole song, never even sneaking a peek to see if anyone was watching.

If you've ever told anyone that "it was all a blur," you'll know how it was for me singing that song. I don't remember much about it other than when I was done, there was a huge rush of adrenaline along with a real sense of accomplishment. In fact, it was almost like a dream, but it was real! I had just sung karaoke for the first time, and also faced my fear of singing and being in front of a crowd.

I put the microphone back in the mic holder as the small group of people in the room were clapping their hands. That applause was for my singing! My brother Ashton hollered out, "You did it, Eric!"

As I went back to my seat a lady came up to me, crying. She was a bit intoxicated and also very emotional because of the attacks at home. She hugged me and said, "Honey, you need to go home and be a singer. You need to pursue this 'cause you are good!"

Flash forward a few years, and I am standing in the office of one of the nation's most famous vocal coaches in Los Angeles, California. He also confirmed that I would have a successful career as a singer—if I chose to put in the effort. So, I went to work. Over the years I would play hundreds of concerts and sell thousands of CDs worldwide. I remember the first time hearing one of my songs played on a large national radio station, and the first time seeing my picture in national magazines. To this day it still feels like I am living in a dream. If you want to learn more about my music career go to ericdodge.com.

The cruise ship. First picture of me singing, 9-11-2001.

My cowboy Grandpa Dodge and my dog Molly. My song,
"The Last Real Cowboy" was about him.

12 NEVER GIVE UP

"If you are going through hell, keep going."
—Winston S. Churchill

Much of my life story comes from my years as an aspiring country singer. This life was far from what I wanted to be growing up. In my teens and early adult years I couldn't be more scared of standing on a stage. And it's true that I still get nervous and scared, but I look at it as validation that I'm doing just what I'm supposed to be doing.

When I was younger I needed a reading and writing tutor because I was not good at either of those subjects. Later on I ended up dropping out of college with bad grades plus social anxiety and depression problems. But here I am writing my second book, when I am far from being an academically gifted person. You see, my theme of *Why Not Today* goes very deep for me. My message of Face Your Fears and Chase Your Dreams is something I am very passionate about. I always tell people that you have two choices: you can fight, or give up.

There are many times I wanted to give up. I sure thought about it. If you read some of my old journals you would be shocked at how depressed I was. In those journals I wrote almost suicide-sounding notes to myself. Once I wrote my own obituary, just to see how I wanted to be remembered. This is hard for me to say, but it's the truth. I know how it feels to be suicidal, and I know that some of you have felt this way. I encourage you to fight. Never give up.

I have not fit into any easy category in my life. I am kind of a desperado or a trail forger, and at times that has been very lonely. I make my own path in all that I do. I am a singer who doesn't play guitar or write songs very well. I am terrible at reading and writing and yet I am writing a book. I grew up in a community where you are expected to get married at a young age, and I did not. My religion was very forward on wanting young men to serve religious missions, and I did not. I didn't fit in at college, or school. I tried karate and martial arts and was not that great at it. I never had roommates, I never moved away from the town I grew up in. I can go on and on and on about me not fitting in and not following the crowd. I just don't do things the traditional way. I've always forged my own path and done what felt right to me.

I never gave up; I only moved on. I now know that this is a good quality. All that I went through was because I wanted to fit the mold, but I could not. Now I know how great it is that I don't fit in. Even when I started to write this book I had people tell me it was a bad idea. One of my friends said I shouldn't write it because it may be too personal. She thought that being too personal was a bad idea. When she found out I was almost done writing it, she said, "Writing the book despite others' advice, huh?"

To which I replied, "That's just me—I feel like it needs to be written." Once I started to write this book it poured out of me, and I could not stop until it was done.

Now that I'm a member of the National Speakers Association I speak to audiences in many different industries. Yes, I always use my music in my presentations, but there are messages in between the songs. I speak to youth on my experiences with bullying as well as adults on my experiences with depression and inner bullying. Some of my speaking events are for health, mental health, and weight loss groups. I also speak to many groups of aspiring singers and musicians and the entertainment industry. Most people I talk to seem to have one thing in common: they all have fears that need to be faced in order to achieve their dreams.

One particular speech, I was going over some of my marketing ideas and things I had tried in my music career that most people would never try, relating some of the fears and trials I'd faced. I was hands-on, showing them marketing ideas, old CDs I'd made locally, newspaper articles, and much more. This was because many of the audience members wanted a career in music, and I thought it would be great to really dig in with my failures and successes. Some of the items were downright embarrassing, but I felt I needed to share. And there is one of my favorites that I want to share with you now. I feel like it's important.

You see, I wouldn't be here today without others supporting me. So many times we fail to achieve our potential, or we fail to chase our dreams because we fear. We fear failure, rejection, or just have plain old self-doubt. From day one, I had people who cheered me on. Even now, looking back, it's clear that I wasn't at the level I thought I was at the time, but because of my supporters I pushed through and got better! Family and friends helped me to believe in myself when I needed it the most.

Here's the story. At that time I was fairly new at singing. The first year I started to sing, I had tried out for a local contest. Whoever won this contest got radio airplay, newspaper press, and got so much publicity that I *really* wanted to win this thing! Well, the first year I didn't win, and actually came in 8th out of 8 in the final round. The next year I worked really hard, hired performance coaches, vocal coaches, and took every opportunity to perform. I also made friends with a songwriter and helped co-write my first song, called "It Ain't Love."

The next year I felt ready, so I tried out for the contest again. I made it through all the rounds and got to the finale. I felt so prepared and did my best job. When the announcer called out that I had actually won this contest, I was so excited! *This is it*, I said to myself. *I finally got my big break!*

Cheers, hugs, and high-fives all around afterwards. It was so amazing being a new singer and experiencing this feeling. From seeing how it went for past winners, I knew that the next day the radio station would be playing my song, my name would be announced for days on end, and my career in music would finally kick into gear!

Well, as the next day arrived and I listened eagerly to the radio, I never heard a mention of my name. I thought surely it would be the following day, so I'd be patient, and then it would be in the paper as well. Well, on Day 2 there was still no mention anywhere of me winning this contest. I was concerned, and emailed the station manager asking him what was going on. He messaged me back, and asked me to call him ASAP. So I rang him up and learned that my win was surrounded by accusations and scandal. Some of the other contestants had complained and threatened to take action against the radio station if they gave me any publicity! *What?*

The station manager informed me they had to re-count the scores since some of the judges knew me. So they threw out the scores from the high and the low judge, and I still won the contest by those numbers.

The next accusation was that I had not written my song, that it was not an original, and that I shouldn't have gotten the extra points for that. I remember crying over this and feeling hurt and angry. I called up the songwriter I'd collaborated with, and he offered to call the station and set the record straight. He did call, and the station said they were OK with me being the winner, but would definitely not announce it or play my song, just to be safe.

This was terrible! Why had this happened? I was crushed.

But a few days later, there was a nice big article in the paper about me winning, and even a picture of me from the contest. I was so happy to see that they had let the accusations go. Only quite a while later did I learn that my family was responsible! They had paid for and placed the ad. They wanted me to have the recognition I earned, and were so upset at how everything had gone, that they literally designed and paid for an ad in the local newspaper.

Out of all the articles I've gotten, this one will always be the most cherished and most important. Thank you to my family, my friends, and my supporters over the years. The last line in the song "Just One Person" from the Broadway musical *Snoopy*, as well as on my *Fork In The Road* CD says, "And when all those people believe in you, Deep enough and strong enough believe in you, Hard enough and long enough, it stands to reason you Yourself will start to see what everybody sees in you. And maybe even you, can believe in you, too."

Please don't ever give up on your dreams. Please support those around you in need of support.

I've been booed on the stage. I have been threatened. I have had some of the nastiest emails you have ever seen sent to me. I've had terrible phone calls, and had my house defiled with terrible profanities. But you know you are making a difference when people go out of their way to try and stop you. Don't stop. Keep going, and never quit. It is always easier to quit. Surround yourself with support and go for it. Face your fears and chase your dreams, and remember to never give up.

My mother got one of her favorite sayings from the Disney movie *Finding Nemo*. She always says, "Just keep swimming." There's a little piece of paper on the dash of my truck to remind me to never give up, and **just keep swimming**.

13 WHEN THINGS GO WRONG

"Character cannot be developed in ease and quiet.
Only through experience of trial and suffering can the soul be
strengthened, ambition inspired, and success achieved."
—Helen Keller

The name of this chapter says it all. It doesn't say *if* things go wrong. It says WHEN things go wrong, and go wrong they will. I used to believe nothing could ever go wrong, but then it did.

The day I got the phone call saying my sister and nephew had been in a horrific accident on the freeway, sheer terror swept over me. There was so much fear that my mind could not concentrate. They said, "Come to the hospital, but everyone is just fine."

Then on the way to the hospital, I hear that Life Flight has been called to take my 4-month-old nephew Daegon to Las Vegas for brain injuries; that his mother can't go because she was hospitalized for a broken pelvis. Well, Life Flight doesn't take to the air for "just fine."

The news got worse and worse. The driver—our neighbor and friend—had coded, and they were trying to revive her as we spoke. This was a nightmare; a nightmare I have had over and over again, since my biggest fear is that of losing loved ones.

When the first call came I was watching a movie on the couch. I was relaxed and life was good, but one phone call of less than 30 seconds can change everything. At the time of the accident, my sister's husband was nowhere to be found. She couldn't fly with my nephew to get his emergency brain shunt put in place, and we couldn't find her husband to sign the papers to allow this procedure to be done!

When the Las Vegas hospital called to ask my sister if she could get ahold of him, she could not, and none of us could. Mom and Dad were watching my sister Emily and helping her to recover, so they couldn't go to Las Vegas.

Emily gave her permission for her son's surgery via phone, but she could not even be there with him. Then her husband was finally located. He'd been out of town but came back immediately when he heard the news. This was a complete nightmare. Talk about anxiety and panic attacks! There was nothing for me to do and I felt helpless.

As far as everyone's injuries went, those things had improved a little. My sister was released to my parents' house for six weeks of bed rest. The woman driving the car had been brought back to life and was stable with a broken neck, ribs, punctured lung, and more serious internal injuries. Little Daegon was stable in a Las Vegas intensive care unit with a fractured skull and brain swelling.

Emily and her family actually lived in Las Vegas, but her husband was out of town so much that she had all the mail forwarded to our family home in Utah while she recovered.

One day I was at the house helping her sort through her family's bills. Looking over a credit card statement, she noticed a charge for a bunch of flowers. She asked us if any flowers had been delivered to her at the hospital or at the house, but we hadn't noticed any flowers anywhere. There were no flowers in Daegon's ICU room either. Then she noticed that this florist was in another city, in another state. Emily went white as a ghost and just sat there a moment. Then she called her husband. *"Honey, who are the flowers for?"*

Usually secrets are not hidden forever, and the reality about her husband and where he'd been when Daegon was in intensive care needing a desperate brain shunt had come into the light. This affair had been going on for some time, but my sister was totally unaware of it. That day I'd learn how terrible it was to see Emily completely crushed and defeated. She was just broken.

The divorce came very quick after that. In a matter of weeks Emily went from having the dream marriage she'd always wanted, to being in a hospital bed in Utah with her son in a Las Vegas hospital, and her marriage falling completely apart. This was a whirlwind of a time for our family. Things eventually got better, but never did go back quite the same. However, my sister is a very tough girl and she rose above this trial.

Over the next several years our family would go through many more trials. My dad and mom would both have major health scares, and my mother went to a wellness rehab center for an entire summer. I'd lose other grandparents and a dear aunt to death. And there would be more broken families. But most of these trials have led to great periods of growth. **Life will go wrong, and life will go on**. It's just bound to happen. The more I go through life the more I appreciate and love my family.

I am a protector, and always wish I could do more, but most of the time it's something completely out of my control. If only I could turn into that superhero I always wanted to be as a kid, and make things right when they go wrong.

We all have stories like these in our lives. But it's not what went wrong that we need to worry about, it's how we deal with it. We have the choice to either crumble under the pain and the fear, or rise above it. Yes, we can let it make us stronger or we can crumble. I know that it has made me stronger, because these things don't define me.

Mom and Dad have made me so proud for all they've done with the trials they have faced. I am so proud of my sister and brothers as well, for all they have gone through. All three of my siblings and their families have faced their own huge trials, and I stand in awe of their resilience.

My surviving grandmother faced many hardships as well, and is still living an incredible life. I love to hear her stories of growing up in a time when her house had no plumbing, no power, and no running water. In her town they drove wagons with horses. They milked cows and traded for food. It was a very different time, and her stories make it come alive.

With a very solid family foundation, I know how lucky I am. Some people do not know how that feels. Some have completely different trials and pains, and many are worse than I can imagine. Often, people deal with these trials with such courage and strength that I can't help but be inspired. *You* are my hero. So when things go wrong, please don't let it define you.

I once heard it said that we have to experience the downs to enjoy the ups; that without darkness there would be no light and without sadness there would be no happiness. So choose happiness. Enjoy the ride, all of it.

As my mother was lying in a hospital bed fighting for her life, I remember us having a wonderful conversation on the phone. You see, she was severely overweight and had many health problems. Mom told me, "I'm going to get healthy and get out of here. I'm going to come home, and we are going to start hiking all over those mountains! There are many places I want to see still and I'm not done yet. You just wait and see what this old lady can do."

Well, she surprised everyone when she lost that 130 pounds and did her second half marathon when she was 60 years old. By now she has probably hiked more miles and more trails than I have. Mom has proven to our entire family that anything is possible. Things can go wrong—but oh, things can go so right if you really work for it!

My mom meant what she said—130 pounds lost.

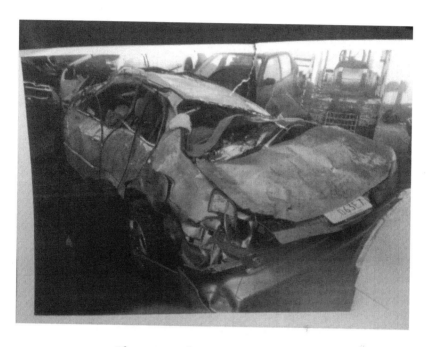

The car my sister and nephew were in.

14　WHY NOT TODAY?

"The timeless in you is aware of life's timelessness. And knows that
yesterday is but today's memory and tomorrow is today's dream."
　　　　　　　　　　　　—Kahlil Gibran, *The Prophet*

Being a traveling singer and speaker, I have experienced many things.
Different concerts, towns, travel situations, all of it. There are also stories
behind the songs I sing, and I love sharing them from the stage. I have
amazing writers and co-writers that have become my friends. My music
career would not be what it is without my friends Amy Lacey, Marla
Cilley, Andy Dodge, my band, my friends, and of course my very
supportive Mom and Dad and family. My life has certainly changed since
I have become a singer and a speaker.

　　As mentioned in other chapters, I know what being severely
depressed feels like. I know what severe anxiety and panic attacks feel
like. I know what seasonal depression is. I've felt post-holiday depression
and post-surgery depression. I know what it is to feel down. Now, some
people can relate to this and others cannot. Most people that know me
would never think in a million years that I'd know what suicidal feelings
were. Some people talk about others who take their own lives and call
them selfish, and say things like, "How could someone ever think like
that?" or "I could never relate to someone who thinks like that."

　　When I was overweight, depressed, and had low self-esteem, I felt
every bit of that. I know how it feels to turn to substances such as alcohol
to calm your nerves and numb your sadness and pain. I've witnessed
firsthand a family member going through rehab, and I've been to
Alcoholics Anonymous and Narcotics Anonymous. I've seen all of these
effects and been very involved in them. I myself have turned to alcohol

before, and very large amounts of it, when I was feeling down.

Depression is real. It's not a made-up thing. It can be very debilitating, and can control and destroy your life. Some people are insensitive to this and don't understand it because they haven't experienced it. But the good news is that you can fight back! I did, and changed my entire life.

I found purpose and passion in my life even though I've witnessed horrific divorces, terrible car accidents, and broken families, all in my very immediate family. I have seen so much sadness, but also resilience, in the eyes of my own family members, and have learned so much from them.

From one of my mentors I learned that when your WHY is powerful enough, your HOW will become clear. Meaning that when you have a good enough reason to change your life, how you will make it happen will become visible.

So what do you want to change or do? Do you want to be happy? Lose weight? Have more money? Try new things? Make more friends? Become more spiritual? Have an amazing relationship? Read more books? What is it?

Make a list of all the things you want. Really sit down and just write this list out. Set yourself up for some uninterrupted time and just write. Dream like you have never dreamed before. Just pretend that what you write on that paper will all come true. You really have nothing to lose here. Pick your most important 1 to 3 dreams or goals, and start some small actions that will help you meet them.

Don't put this off! There is no better day to begin dreaming than right now, because you *can* create the life of your dreams.

At least once a month I try to do things that make me uncomfortable; sometimes even once a week. By stepping out of my comfort zone I grow. Here are some examples:

- When I was in debt I started a budget. I listened to different financial authors and coaches, and studied finance.
- When I was depressed I researched positive quotations and listened to many motivational books on happiness.

- When I wanted to lose weight and get healthier, I tracked my food and calories and upped my activity level. Trying many diets and lifestyle changes, I finally found the one that worked perfectly for me. Losing 80 pounds was one long and grueling process, but I did it.

Just because I wrote down what I wanted, I didn't just assume it would happen. After making my decisions I worked hard at fulfilling them. Taking small steps every day over the course of time ultimately changed my life. Small steps are much easier than drastic changes.

There's a very helpful book called *The Compound Effect,* by my mentor Darren Hardy. It is all about making small changes. This book changed my life and it can help change yours. Ask yourself, Why Not Today?

I'd like to end this chapter with the lyrics to the song "Why Not Today," written by Amy Lacey for Marla Cilley, The FlyLady. After we met in a TV studio many years ago, Marla asked me to be the singer for this song. The song fit my life to a T, and Marla felt the song was meant for me. After recording it, we found that it was meant for many people worldwide! It became a best selling album and thousands of CDs were sent all over the world.

"Why Not Today," by Amy Lacey

I've been waiting for just the right moment
for the courage to follow my dreams
But I finally discovered the power lies inside of me
It hit me today there's no better time to begin
This day I've been given is my day to start living so I'm jumping in

Why Not Today while the sun is shining today while I know I can
The past is behind me tomorrow can't find me till I live today
Why not today while my heart is ready today while it's in my grasp
If I start out slowly I'm confident knowing I'm still on my way
Why Not Today!

I've been searching in all the wrong places
for the courage to follow my dreams
But I finally discovered the power lies inside of me
I could spend my life waiting for something to show me the way
But I would be missing the wonderful blessing of embracing today

Why Not Today while the sun is shining today while I know I can
The past is behind me tomorrow can't find me till I live today
Why not today while my heart is ready today while it's in my grasp
If I start out slowly I'm confident knowing I'm still on my way
Why Not Today!

I'm ready, I'm willing, I'm able, I'm learning to fly,
But how will I know how high I can soar if I never try

Why Not Today while the sun is shining today while I know I can
The past is behind me tomorrow can't find me till I live today
Why not today while my heart is ready today while it's in my grasp
If I start out slowly I'm confident knowing I'm still on my way
Why Not Today!

For the full music and lyrics, check it out online. Go to ericdodge.com.

15   BREAK FREE

"Yesterday is gone. Tomorrow has not yet come.
We have only today. Let us begin."
—Mother Teresa

It's time—right now. I want you to do something that I learned at a fire walking ceremony you'll read about later. I want you to write down all of the things that you are scared of.

What in your past are you ashamed of? Embarrassed about? Who are you angry with? What regrets do you have? Write them all down on a piece of paper, and don't leave any of them out.

Are you scared of spiders, death, germs, the dark? Are you angry with a sibling or a child, or about the years you feel you wasted doing nothing? Write it all down. Fill up as many pieces of paper as you have to. And then, I want you to take that paper and burn it. Start yourself a nice campfire and throw it all in there. Watch the smoke carry all your worries and fears away. You see, you have to break free and let it all go. There is nothing we can do about all that. It is in the past.

Our past should not have the power to control our future. However, I have let this happen to me on more than one occasion. I've passed up amazing relationships, amazing friendships, great opportunities, and great memories, all because I stopped trusting and started protecting myself. I needed to break free from those feelings and those emotions a long time ago.

If you don't want to start a fire, then just write it all in the sand on a beach with your finger and let the waves pull all your worries out to sea. Or write it on paper and then put it through a shredder.

First, tell yourself that you deserve to let it all go and break free from it. Tell yourself that you deserve to forgive yourself and others. Give yourself permission to be happy. And right now is the time. Don't wait another second! This is the first step to moving beyond your past and to finally *Break Free*. I sing a song called "Break Free," and it is about this exact message.

Check out the song "Break Free" by Amy Lacey, myself, and Natalie Johnson. Here are the lyrics.

"Break Free," by Amy Lacey, Eric Dodge, Natalie Johnson

The enemy will tell you
You're too weak to change
You belong in misery
Tied up in these chains
But something burns within you
That makes you want to try
You wonder if you've got the strength
To break these chains and fly
Face your demons
Find your reasons
Start believin'
You are strong inside

Break free
From the past that leaves you haunted
Break free
From the fear that ties you down
Break free
And live the life you've wanted
You are not a prisoner
You were meant to be
Free

A better life is waiting just outside the door
It's time to show the world you're not a victim anymore
The moment you've got power is the moment you decide
Are you gonna give up now or are you gonna fight?
Face your demons
Find your reasons
Start believin'

You are strong inside

Break free
From the past that leaves you haunted
Break free
From fear that ties you down
Break free
And live the life you've wanted
You are not a prisoner
You were meant to be
Free
Break free

Face your demons
Find your reasons
Start believin'
You are strong inside

Break free
From the past that leaves you haunted
Break free
From fear that ties you down
Break free
And live the life you've wanted
You are not a prisoner
You were meant to be

You are not a prisoner
You were meant to be

Free

Check out ericdodge.com for the full song.

16 DON'T MISS THE GOOD STUFF

"You make your choices, and then your choices make you."
—Darren Hardy, *The Compound Effect*

You see, when I first started as a singer and met Marla Cilley, The FlyLady, I traveled all over the United States singing songs during her keynote speeches. Back then I had no idea how to speak and no idea how to captivate an audience like that, other than by using my music and lyrics. Marla would speak for a few minutes then ask me to come up and sing a song. We would trade back and forth throughout the speech for close to an hour. Then we'd set up a meet-and-greet and everyone would come up to meet Marla. Sometimes the line would consist of hundreds of people, and the wait to meet her would be several hours!

This was amazing to me. I couldn't believe all these people would pack a room and then wait for hours to meet someone. Marla wasn't a rock star; she wasn't a famous political figure, and she wasn't even well known outside of her own circle. She was just someone who was helping other people—a whole lot of other people. Marla *was* a rock star to her own circle.

This was the first time I'd seen anything like this. Marla was not on any radio stations, she wasn't hosting her own TV talk show, yet millions of people knew who she was. She had sold so many copies of her book that I could not even comprehend it. My few thousand CDs I'd sold at the time were nothing to her hundreds of thousands of books!

I got to spend a lot of time with Marla and got to know her very well. We became like family. She'd even come and stay with us at home, and I'd go out to North Carolina and stay with Marla and her husband Robert. Marla became a friend and a mentor, and I learned a whole lot about the speaking world through her sharing. It was so wonderful how she could motivate and help people!

This caused me to start making major changes in my musical direction. I didn't want to play at bars and dance halls anymore, and suddenly I didn't care if I was on the radio either—I just wanted to make a difference and help people.

Marla helped me produce some of my music and albums. She and my parents, as well as brother Andy, went to Nashville and recorded my *Why Not Today* CD. That will always be one of my most cherished memories.

Over the years of knowing Marla I got to know other amazing people. Marla started bringing other speakers along with us to events where I would sing. One guy was named Jonathan Roche. Jonathan is a fitness guru with a message about health and wellness. He and I became great friends as well, and he'd give me tips and tricks to improve my health and wellness. Jonathan and Marla sort of became my mental and physical health team!

Several years ago Jonathan gave me a subscription to *Success Magazine*. I loved reading all the stories of amazing inspirational people. The subscription came with a free audio CD, and it was great to listen to and learn from all those people as well.

Success Magazine quickly became my favorite inspirational material. I signed up for a multi-year subscription and still get it today; probably always will. The publisher of this magazine is a speaking and entrepreneurial rock star named Darren Hardy. Darren quickly rose to be one of my top mentors, and I bought every book and program he suggested. I loved listening to all this stuff, and would try hard to apply it to my music business.

For some reason I was so drawn to all the speakers, and would marvel at Jim Rohn, Zig Ziglar, John C. Maxwell, Joel Osteen, and the list can go on and on. I loved the messages and the way I felt after listening, and wanted to leave my audiences feeling this same way after my concerts!

Next up, I hired a business coach. She was asking me questions one day when I told her I wanted to be a life coach to help mentor others. Well, she continued to grill me and asked, "Do you like teaching voice lessons to others?"

I answered *no* with zero reservations.

Then she asked, "Do you see yourself working one-on-one with people for hours on end, or do you see yourself on a stage delivering a powerful message to a group?"

"Hmm, definitely not the one-on-one thing," I said. "That would be hard on me emotionally."

And I'll never forget what she said next. "Eric my friend, what you want to be is a *keynote speaker,* only with your music."

That sank into my mind, and I pictured myself speaking on stage. Not only singing, but speaking!

My business manager then asked me about my goals. Since I had them written down I shared one with her. Word for word, the goal was, "I want to create a new model for my music that can make it sustainable for my entire lifetime, and not feel the pressures of the regular music industry."

"Bingo!" she said. "You already know what you need to do."

And she was right, I *was* on the right path. For some reason, and I believe this goes for all of us, our lives are already in motion and the door that we need to walk through is right in front of us. We need only to turn the knob and step through that door. We need to recognize these doors in our lives.

A few weeks later I was at a fair expo, selling my country music act against several other artists who were doing the same thing. It was very frustrating because it was all a big popularity contest, and none of our content mattered. All that I had put into my messages and all that I had created to help other people was muddied down by a whole group of other entertainers who were selling on price, and selling that they could play cover songs for hours on end.

This was definitely not the right place for me. I didn't want to copy other successful bands by playing their songs. I wanted to leave my friends and fans feeling uplifted and hopeful. I wanted to help people see that they could leave my show and feel like they could accomplish anything. But now, I was having to fight on price.

Then a guy I'd never seen before jumped up on stage and began an amazing keynote speech. He was up there for an hour speaking and doing magic tricks to support his messages, and I was captivated. He made me feel like I could do anything. He was there to speak to the fair personnel, but it seemed he was speaking right to me.

As soon as he got off the stage I rushed over to meet him. His name was Brad Barton. We quickly became friends and Brad became one of my mentors, and my key to joining the National Speakers Association. Because of Brad I've met so many wonderful people.

I'd also heard of and seen this amazing entertainer named Jason Hewlett around, but he was so far out of my league I'd never talked with him. He was a big-shot Las Vegas entertainer making bank in the entertainment world.

Many people would tell me, "Hey, maybe someday you'll be as successful as Jason Hewlett. You know he makes *this much* at every fair he plays, right? You know he doesn't have to split it with a band, right?"

Not knowing Jason personally, I must admit feeling some jealousy. I wanted to be successful like he was, and to be doing my music full time. I wanted to win a CMA award and be able to reach millions of people like Marla and Jason—I just didn't know how.

Through Brad Barton I ended up in the same National Speakers Association chapter as Jason Hewlett. I sat by him at an event and got to know him. Jason was so nice and friendly. He offered me all kinds of advice and friendship, and quickly joined the ranks of my biggest mentors.

Like always, I decided that instead of working my way up from the bottom, I'll just jump in and see where the chips fall. So I signed up for my first National Convention of the National Speakers Association in Philadelphia. Since I didn't know anyone who was going, I posted on an online group that I'd be joining everyone at the convention, and that I hoped to meet people.

Immediately a lady named Laurie Guest sent me a message on Facebook. Laurie was so nice, and asked if I wanted to call her for any advice. Over the years of dealing with some very interesting people online, I learned that you never call people back because they always want something from you. This lady obviously wanted something from me, so I was not going to call her. We messaged back and forth for a while, and she gave up on trying to get me to call her. Her last message was that she'd watch for me at the convention.

I flew across the country all alone, nervously, and embarked on my first ever National Speakers Association convention. I wasn't even there for an hour when a lady grabbed me by the arm as I came off the escalator.

"Are you Eric Dodge?" she questioned.

That was Laurie! She had found me right off. Laurie showed me where to register and helped me find my way around. She invited me to sit at her table for meals and she introduced me to people. She really went above and beyond to help me, so I just knew something was coming. I just knew that she was being overly nice because she *wanted something*.

Then I finally realized what it was. She did want something—my friendship. Laurie wanted nothing more from me than that.

Laurie has been and will always be instrumental in my life. She took my arm and showed me the way when I needed someone the most.

Because I have been honored to meet and work with so many outstanding mentors I now do musical keynote events for many different organizations. Yes, my life was forever changed when I began traveling the country with a keynote speaker named Marla Cilley.

"Things done imperfectly still bless our lives."
— Marla Cilley, *Sink Reflections*

On one of the monthly *Success Magazine* audio CDs, Darren Hardy introduced a speaker and author named Scott McKain. Darren was interviewing him about one of his new books. While making arrangements to travel to one of Darren Hardy's weekend presentations in California, I decided to first make a stop in Las Vegas to see Scott speak at a chapter event for the National Speakers Association. This weekend would change my life once again.

As Scott was wrapping up an incredible speech about being unique and standing out, about creating distinction in your life, he put a picture of a beautiful sunset up on the screen. Scott said, "I know I've stood here and talked to you about working hard and giving it your all, but I want to remind you to slow down and enjoy the ride. I want you to make sure you don't miss the good stuff along the way. You see, this picture of the sunset you're looking at is the last picture I ever took with my wife Sheri. She passed away from cancer just after this trip. She was so worried that nobody would remember her after she died. Just promise me that you don't miss the good stuff."

This was a very powerful speech and a very powerful photo. It got me thinking about how much I was missing. Picturing myself at the end of my life, would I have lived up to my potential? Would I feel like a success or a failure? How *was* I living my life? What could I do to feel like a success? These were the questions that were running through my mind, and in response, Amy, Natalie and I sat down and wrote a song called "Don't Miss The Good Stuff." It was based on all of our experiences with these same questions.

So, be grateful. Be happy with what you have. You may have had some terrible blows in your life. You may be in a hurry to get where you are going. Slow Down. We are all going to get to our final destination someday, no matter what we do. Let's enjoy this ride. Let's live up to our potential. Promise me that you don't miss the good stuff!

"Don't Miss The Good Stuff,"
by Amy Lacey, Eric Dodge, Natalie Johnson

Have you ever seen a sunset, like a fire burning in the sky?
You're the only one who sees it the rest of the world passes by
You stare in wonder at that painting in the sky
And you see those colors above you, so glad to be alive

Don't miss the good stuff
Don't miss the good stuff
The best things will pass if you go through life too fast
Don't miss the good stuff
Take time for the good stuff
Soak it up live it up every moment life is made of
Don't miss the good stuff

Sittin' round a campfire on a night you wish would never end
You laugh and sing your favorite songs with all of your best friends
And you feel that music reaching deep down in your soul
And you pause for a minute thinking this is what life is for

Don't miss the good stuff
Don't miss the good stuff
The best things will pass if you go through life too fast
Don't miss the good stuff
Take time for the good stuff
Soak it up live it up every moment life is made of
Don't miss the good stuff.

Every laugh, every tear, add up to those moments
that make me glad I'm here

Don't miss the good stuff

Don't miss the good stuff
The best things will pass if you go through life too fast
Don't miss the good stuff
Take time for the good stuff
Soak it up, live it up, every moment life is made of
Don't miss the good stuff

Go to ericdodge.com for full song.

17 I WALKED ON FIRE

"Neither fire nor wind, birth nor death can erase our good deeds."
—the Buddha

One of the best things for beating depression is setting clear goals, and having some sort of direction. This realization has been huge for me. Every year I set goals and resolutions. One that is very common for me is to continually face my fears. I may fail at times, but at least I try. A good number of these goals are accomplished, especially at the beginning of the year when I am all charged up and ready to go.

So a few years ago, after listening to a very life-changing book called *The 18 Rules of Happiness* by Karl Moore, I decided to try new things every year. If you want to learn to be more happy, I highly recommend this book.

One of Karl's rules is to say *yes* more, so I planned to do this. I wanted to live more adventures, and to take more chances. This was kind of my theme for the year—to face my fears and do things I wouldn't normally do.

I'd decided to do this all right, but I wasn't doing very well! One night I was at the house having a good old-fashioned pity party, stretched out on the couch watching TV. At about 5:10 p.m. I was doing a little time-wasting on Facebook, just wishing for something fun to do. There was this little tab on Facebook that said "events" next to it, so I decided to check and see what events were happening around town. Maybe I could talk myself into going and checking one of them out.

Well, the first event to come up said Fire Walk. That grabbed my attention fast. I'd seen these on reality TV shows and heard about people who had walked on hot burning coals barefoot, but I had sure never been to one. This thing started in 20 minutes.

Should I go, should I not go, should I go? This argument went back and forth in my head and for some reason I decided to pull myself off the couch. It would surely be interesting, and I could just watch other people walk on the coals and leave at any time. No one could force you to do something like that.

Walking out to my truck I didn't notice the cold much, but when I got to the event it was windy and freezing outside. There wasn't exactly a crowd, but I recognized a few people so I started talking to them. These folks talked me into staying, but told me that once it started there was no leaving until it was all over.

Trust me, I was really worked up over that fact and wanted to sneak out! But then they asked if I'd help with the firewood and load it up in my truck. I couldn't resist helping with that simple task, but now I was really stuck with these crazy fire people. There was no escape at that point, so I decided to stay and make the best of it somehow.

I became involved in every step of the process. I helped build the fire; I helped prepare the fire. We were all asked to write down our biggest fears on a 3×5 card, and once the fire was burning good, to throw the cards into the flames. Now you know where I got that suggestion from earlier in the book, when I mentioned burning your fears.

We had several team building exercises where we told complete strangers what we thought their gifts were, just by how they made us feel on first impressions. We each told the group how we came to be at this event. The whole group laughed when I said, "I was lying on the couch and saw this event on Facebook."

I told the others how my New Year's resolution was to try things I would not normally try, and that this was very much something I had never seen before.

The instructor told us that our minds had to be right to walk on the coals. The flames leaping up in the darkness had nothing to do with a friendly little campfire! This thing was a huge bonfire and it was super-hot, so hot I could barely stand next to it. At this point I had zero plans to walk across and made it very clear that I was just there to watch.

As time passed and the flames got closer to being only coals, they spread out water-soaked carpet on all four sides of the fire. They then invited us all to remove our shoes and socks, saying that this in no way meant we had to walk across, and that if we weren't in the right frame of mind it was highly possible to get burned.

The instructor told us that many times the fears that we see or feel before walking across the coals are very real. It's not just fear about the coals and getting burnt, but fears that are really big in our own lives.

At that point I was standing there with my shoes and socks off, freezing in the night air, especially with the water-soaked icy cold carpet under my bare feet. A lady looked up at me and asked, "Are you going to walk?"

"No, I'm not going to!" I responded. "I don't want to get burned, and I already know what my fears are!"

I heard the instructor say, "The coals are ready, and I invite any of you who feel like you are ready to cross the coals. What's on the other side of these coals that you need to cross for? Don't look down, look past the coals, and just tell yourself what you need to get past in your life."

That hit me hard. How could I go home and say I had spent three hours of my evening freezing in the dark across from a roaring bonfire, getting prepared to cross hot coals, and then not even try it? That would haunt me for the rest of my life.

I talked to myself mentally, saying, *why don't you just cross the coals? Even if it burned you, at least you can say you tried.*

I was still fighting myself, and just then the first person stepped forward and crossed that red-hot bed of coals! His face and whole body posture looked so determined, and he never glanced down.

That guy didn't need to see anyone do it first! A twinge of jealousy stabbed at me because he had just trusted that it could be done, and he went for it all on his own courage. Then I beat myself up more that I didn't trust the leader of the group. I didn't even fully trust that the guy I just saw cross the coals wasn't in fact burned.

Then a few others crossed! There were cheers and hugs and people crying on the other side of the fire. They were saying over and over that they weren't burned!

Wait—maybe this was just a big trick, that they were all in on it. It had to be! Maybe the lesson was that you *did* get burned, and that you were to go home and think about how it hurt, but of course it was worth the pain to cross and beat that mental hurdle.

Despite thinking this was a scam, I felt myself inching closer and closer to the coals.

An unknown voice called out from somewhere, "Are you going to go?"

"No way," I said loudly, "but I want to stand up here and at least look at it."

A few people stood next to me and offered to walk with me. Looking closely at the coals you could see a few darker spots where people's feet had dampened the heat. Maybe I could just step on those spots.

But just then a gust of wind hit and the coals fired up, glowing intensely! I stalled to see if the red-orange surface would start to cool off, and my heart started pounding. And then I heard these words in my head: *Eric, you never finish anything. You chicken out at the very last minute and you don't trust anyone. You made it this far and the worst thing that can happen is your feet will burn. However, if you quit and walk away now, you failed.*

My head was in a huge turmoil and I felt a real panic attack coming on. I wanted to run off from that fire in any direction, hopefully towards my truck.

Yes, my New Year's resolution was to try new things. I was here, I was prepared; I needed to show myself that I don't always quit, and I don't need to trust before jumping. So what if I get burned? Is the pain of burning worse than the pain of regret?

I felt myself step off toward the coals with no turning back, and heard myself saying out loud, "Oh my gosh!! I can't believe I'm doing this!" before my foot even hit the coals.

Pushing ahead, one foot after the other, never looking down, never slowing down, and looking only toward the other side.

I crossed those coals—I did it! I crossed those burning coals and I conquered the inner voice in my head that wanted me to fail. There were cheers, and hugs, and high-fives all around. This was exhilarating and amazing! My feet hurt only a little. They may have been slightly singed, but definitely not burned like I pictured they would be.

Now I know that my fears will always try and control me. I also know that at that moment I didn't listen. I had let that voice whine and cry at me all night that I couldn't do this, but I still crossed those coals. **I accepted the risk of failure over the risk of regret**. The pain of regret is always much stronger then the pain of pushing ahead.

Whatever hot coals may fall into your path, I hope you tell yourself that you have come too far not to cross. Maybe you will get a little bit singed, but it will be so very worth it in the end.

In my journey I've learned so much about myself, and I am keeping my commitment to continue to try new things, even if it seems a little uncomfortable or crazy at first. You never know what kinds of friends you may meet or what kinds of roadblocks you may break through.

I saved one of the coals to remind me of this day.

18 THE JOY IS IN THE PURSUIT

> "Learn how to be happy with what you have
> while you pursue all that you want."
> —Jim Rohn

Do you ever mentally beat yourself up? I'm good at this, are you? You could say I'm a bigger bully to myself than any of the other bullies have been. I can put myself down like no other. I can send my spirits spiraling all the way down in the dumps faster than you can snap your fingers. Looking in the mirror, I can see everything wrong with me within seconds. I talk negatively to myself and can remember all the mistakes I made in the past, feeling pain and guilt over situations I cannot change. Yes, I can hold grudges against myself better than I can hold grudges against anyone else. You see, it is easy for me to put myself down. I can forgive others easily, but it is very hard for me to forgive myself.

I shouldn't have eaten that; I shouldn't have drank that. Well, that was a waste of my time. I shouldn't have said that; I should have done this instead of that. Have you ever done this to yourself? Congratulations, if you have not! Now, let me tell you a story about something that affected me deeply.

I live in a beautiful part of the world. In my many opportunities to see other states and countries during my music career travels, I've seen some amazing scenes! None however compare to the beauty I find in my own backyard, just on the outskirts of Zion National Park in Southern Utah. It's just a few hours from the Grand Canyon, and a few hours from other national parks. Within a 45-minute drive I can be in the mountains filled with pine trees, rivers and lakes, and soaring peaks of over 10,000 feet. There are red rock deserts, arches, and Native American dwellings in my area as well. I kind of feel like I have it all. I'm a very avid outdoorsman, as you may know. I love hiking, camping, horseback adventures, and exploring the area where I live. Though I've been doing this for many years and decades, I still constantly find new and stunning areas.

Just north of my house is a special area called the Red Cliffs Desert Reserve, which is thousands of protected acres of beautiful red rock cliffs and hiking trails. There are endangered tortoises that roam this area as well as many other desert dwelling critters, including the occasional mountain goat, big horn sheep, and mule deer. I love to head out into the deep backcountry of this area and explore the slot canyons and trails. Sometimes I go on foot and sometimes I go on horseback or mountain bike.

Growing up, I had read about the Icehouse Trail. It's a trail that was used many years ago when Southern Utah pioneers used wagons to bring ice down from the higher mountains to use for cooling. I'd heard stories of a neat little dwelling that was used to store this ice, as they would cut the chunks of ice out of the river and transport it to the icehouse.

I wanted to see this icehouse! I imagined it being on a cliffside, overlooking the views of St. George. That's kind of where I'd heard it was, and so one day I set out on foot. I hiked north on one of the trails that supposedly led to this icehouse. After several hours and a few desert tortoises later, I was losing daylight and had yet to find it. I rested for a moment and took in the view, then headed back to my truck.

A few years later I decided to try and get to the icehouse once again. This time I took a route from the west that was supposed to be closer. I should get there in just a few hours. My good friend Glen and I took my dog and headed east on Mesa Rim Trail. About an hour in, we encountered a very angry rattlesnake in the middle of the trail. We also began to run low on water due to the blistering heat we were feeling, and decided to give up for the day.

After a few more attempts with my yellow Labrador Molly before she passed away, and my other yellow Labrador Anna, and never finding the icehouse, it was time to break out the horses. Glen and I saddled up, and set a goal to get to the icehouse this day. We packed our water and snacks, and Anna had her very own dog backpack full of water and dog treats. We were ready, and took off on the closest trail we could find.

The day was fairly warm and the horses were ready to go. I even put a bottle of Diet Coke with lime in my saddlebag for my celebration drink when we found the icehouse. This was going to be the day!

We rode out toward our objective, forging our own trail to cut some time off the trip as we had a lot of ground to cover in a short period of time. We crossed lava fields and sand dunes until we rode up to a fence. The fence was constructed with a spot to easily step over if you were hiking, riding, or doing anything other than driving a motorized vehicle.

The sorrel mare I was riding was named Jessie, and we got along very well together. Glen was riding Kit, kind of a bull-headed chestnut gelding who was not real prone to taking the trails. Kit was used more for arena work and riding, while Jessie was used more for working, ranching and trail riding.

Jessie stepped right over the fence like a champ and into the Red Cliffs Reserve. Well, Kit decided he was not going to step over this fence. It was just not going to happen. Glen did all he could to persuade this horse to cross the fence and he was not having any of it. In fact, the more we both tried the more frustrated and angry Kit began to get. I took Jessie back and forth over the fence in hopes that Kit would see our success and follow our lead, but that didn't work. I tried to lead Kit over as I rode Jessie, and he wasn't impressed with that technique either.

As this battle went from seconds to minutes to over a half-hour, I realized that this was possibly going to stop us from reaching the icehouse. I worked with Kit for a very long time, picking his foot up and setting it on the top rail of the fence, and petting him reassuringly. As he stood by the fence I even tried tossing small pebbles at his behind to get him to step over, but nothing worked. Well, I was as frustrated as Kit was and neither one of us was getting anywhere.

Finally, after more than an hour of trying we got Kit to step over the fence. I ended up having to lay my jacket over the top wood post, setting his foot up on it. Then I lowered his foot down over the other side until it touched solid ground. Once the first foot was over Kit clumsily hopped the other three legs over the fence. We made it! But wow, that was a process. We were all sweaty and tired and so was Kit. I could only hope it didn't take that long going back to our trailer.

With the whole party over the fence, we made our way across a wash and headed for a very steep rocky trail up the mountainside. This was going to be fun for sure! I was filled with anxiety and excitement all mixed together. I had never really ventured this far on horseback, and certainly not with these horses.

We began our ascent up the very steep hill. The horses were slipping and sliding and scrambling their way up the rocky slope. About halfway up, not even at the steepest part yet, I noticed Kit threw a shoe! His foot was not holding up well with the sharp rocks mashing against it.

This was devastating. To press forward would certainly mean damage to Kit's hoof, but to stop and go back would mean one more failed attempt at not finding the icehouse trail.

Who was I kidding? It was time to go back, as we could not chance hurting this horse. But even going back was risky because Kit's hoof was not holding together well, and we did not want to cause any permanent damage.

We dismounted for a short break, ate our snacks, drank our drinks, and then headed back down. Heading back was smooth sailing. It was a beautiful day; the sky was so blue and clear. The horses were behaving and we were really having a great time. Even stepping back over the fence only took half as long on the return. This was a good day.

After that, I tried to hike in from a few more angles without success, and just ended up putting the whole thing on hold.

A few years later I began hiking more and more with my mother. She was on her journey to better health and decided that she was going to start hiking with me. Funny thing was, she came to me one day asking about the Icehouse Trail. She wanted to see the icehouse too, and said, "Since I'm getting older I want to go see this as soon as possible!"

We decided to buy maps and get on the Internet to look at this area with Google Earth. Going back to Mesa Rim Trail, we'd take a stab at the icehouse from the west once again. We figured we probably wouldn't make it, but decided to take the trail and map it all out to determine the best way to get to where the icehouse supposedly was.

Dad was with us too, and we hiked a few miles up the mesa and took in the breathtaking views. We could see the towering snow-covered peaks of Pine Mountain to the north, and the majestic sandstone mesas of Zion National Park to the east. The skies were clear and we could see for miles. I'd never been to this area with my parents before. It was just a great day.

As my parents, my Labrador Anna, and I sat there admiring the peaceful natural beauty, Mom said, "Remember this. You may never be in this place, with these people again. Always remember that as you go on your adventures. Remember who you are with and where you are at." My mom loves to remind us of this whenever we go into an amazing area, which seems to happen often with us.

Well, believe it or not, that day we turned back once again without finding the famous icehouse. How many years had I tried to find it? My imagination had built it up to quite the architectural masterpiece in the mountains. I had to find this structure, and hoped it would be soon. Now that my parents wanted to find it too, I was totally driven to uncover this hidden treasure. I'd been on multiple foot and horseback adventures over the past 15 years; it was high time to find this place!

Dad searched even more online, and Mom found a newer updated map. We now discovered a very rough road that appeared to take us to the north of the Icehouse Trail. I had never attempted this angle before. We'd drive on a bumpy narrow trail for approximately an hour until we reached the parking lot shown on the map. Then we'd hike in the rest of the way. It actually looked much shorter this way, so off we went.

At only 30 minutes in we hit our first snag. The map showed one road coming in from the north to the parking lot, but we had already explored three roads that were not on the map, and somehow none led us anywhere near a parking lot to a trail! After almost an hour of searching we were about to give up. We decided to try one more road that went off through the pine trees, so we took my giant 4-door diesel truck down this little windy and bumpy road. The road led to a burn area where a forest fire had cleared out all the trees. The views exposed by losing the tree cover were amazing, so we stopped and drank it in. We seemed to be very close to the top of the mesa I'd tried to hike to and reach by horseback on multiple occasions, so we had driven almost all the way there!

This was a little sad for me, with all that time spent hiking and riding, and then just driving to the top of the mesa in one hour by finding this Jeep trail on Google Earth! Oh well, none of that mattered since I was close to finding the icehouse, and my parents were with me to celebrate this moment.

We drove as far down the road as we could until it came to a dead end. We got out and began hiking down the mesa to find the trail that I'd hiked and ridden up years before. Within a half-mile we found a single-track trail heading south. This had to be it; this had to be the Icehouse Trail. But we didn't see the icehouse anywhere, so I figured it must be down the trail between this spot and the lower places I had hiked up to before. We'd just need to head down the mesa until we found the icehouse.

Off we went. We saw deer tracks, all kinds of birds, and views that were beyond stunning. I took many pictures. We found a spring in the side of the mountain that filled up a little catch pond for the wildlife to drink from. Anna sure loved jumping in and getting her fill of fresh spring water.

We hiked for a mile or so down the trail and tried to get on our cell phone maps to see if we could find a satellite view of the icehouse, but the cell service was not good in this area, so we were out of luck.

After hiking as far as we could, where we could see down the mesa quite a way, I could just tell that the icehouse was *not* downhill. We must have missed it. I bet that the icehouse was north of where we parked my truck, and that we needed to go the other way. We turned back and hiked all the way back up to the truck.

By this time we were getting tired and a little frustrated that our maps did no good, and that we hadn't seen the icehouse. We decided to separate and pan out to cover the ridge all the way up to the end north of my truck. We each took a section and went looking for the icehouse.

At this point, every stack of lava rocks or pile of tree branches began to look like an icehouse! What did it really look like, where was it, and how could we find it? We looked in the washes and the caves on the cliffs. Maybe it was even further up the mountain. At one point my mom found a pretty large pile of rocks that looked like it could have been an icehouse—a collapsed one—but we just weren't sure.

After several hours of searching it was time to give up. This was hard to do, because I felt we were just so close, and I sure didn't want to give up again. We took lots of pictures and had an amazing day, but headed home without finding our prize.

Soon after we got home I decided to share some pictures with area historians, and ask one of the local explorers to just tell me where the icehouse was.

This expert looked at the pictures and told the story of the icehouse, about how the pioneers used to freeze the water in a spring higher up the mountain and break up the blocks and pieces of ice, then take them down the mountain to the icehouse. Based on the pictures, he said we'd been just about a mile south of the icehouse.

Then he dropped the bombshell. Unfortunately the icehouse was gone, and had been gone for many years. It had collapsed and a road was put over the top of it!

For me this was devastating news. There were so many years of searching and dreaming of the day that I'd finally reach the icehouse. I'd imagined what this house looked like and where it was. I'd gotten so close on so many occasions, now only to find that it doesn't exist anymore, and in my lifetime it never did.

I wallowed in self-pity for several minutes until it hit me like a ton of bricks. *The joy is in the pursuit, the joy was in the journey!* Had I known from day one that this icehouse never existed, I'd have never gone looking for it. I'd have missed out on many experiences; the horseback rides with my friends, the hikes with my two Labrador dogs, the encounter with the rattlesnake. All those trips on foot up the trails with the magnificent views, and the time spent with my friends and family. Look at all the hours I got to enjoy the great outdoors and the company of the people I cared about. This journey provided me with years of memories and stories.

The icehouse may have never existed physically, but it existed in my mind. It was something I desired and pursued. I was not going to give up until I found it. The joy really was in the pursuit. I can no longer be unhappy about what I didn't find—I can be happy about all that I did find along the way. From that day forward I decided to live by the words of my mother, and live by the newfound realization of *take it all in*.

You may never be in this very place, with these very people again. Don't worry about your destination, and find joy in the pursuit and the journey. Whenever I think about that icehouse and those trails, I remind myself that looking for it was not a mistake. None of those adventures in searching for this mystery place was a mistake or a failure. It was all part of the journey. Everything that has happened to you and to me is all part of the journey.

I don't know what it is that you pursue, I only know what I want out of life. I only know what I want to find and what I seek. I know what my "icehouse" is. What's yours? Do you know? Do you seek happiness, joy, health, God, love, or money? Do you have things in your life that you are seeking already?

So how about this, starting right now—stop putting yourself down. Stop looking at your past as a failure or a mistake. Let's stop beating ourselves up and let's remember that the joy is in the pursuit.

What happens when you actually do arrive? Then what? Does the journey just end there? Think about that.

Stop being in such a hurry to reach your destination, because you will surely arrive someday. The destination really doesn't matter as much as the journey.

Do me a favor—look around and tell yourself that you may never be in this exact place surrounded be these exact people again. Take it all in, enjoy the journey, enjoy the pursuit, and by all means stop putting yourself down, because you are incredible!

19 GRATITUDE IS THE KEY

"Let others lead small lives, but not you ...
Let others argue over small things, but not you ...
Let others cry over small hurts, but not you ... Let others leave their
future in someone else's hands, but not you.
—Jim Rohn

What are you grateful for? Are you a glass half-full or glass half-empty
person? Do you constantly think about what is wrong in your life, or what
is wrong in your day? What do you say to yourself when you first wake up
in the morning, or right before you go to bed? These are important
questions to ask.

I'm a big believer in positive thinking and the law of attraction.
I believe in the quotes, "What you think about you bring about," and
"Thoughts are actions." I also believe in karma and paying it forward.

How do you spend your day? I know my day used to be very
different when I was hopeless and depressed. After listening to multiple
audio books on happiness and taking some therapy courses on anxiety
and fear, I learned one of the major keys to happiness and success in my
life. It was gratitude.

I used to want a bigger house, nicer car, millions of dollars, be able
to run a marathon, have a ranch with a trout pond, a beach house in
Hawaii, and many other things. Will these things happen? I don't know.
I am, however, OK with my life now. In fact I am more than OK.

I started something called a gratitude journal. I'm not talking
about just saying *we are thankful for each other* at Thanksgiving time.
I'm talking about really and truly reprogramming your mind to be
grateful and appreciative.

Here are some things I learned from my mentors that helped:

- Listen to audio books all the time. Constantly learn and study the things that you want. Get the top audio books or movies on your desires and learn about them.
- Get a journal; get multiple journals. Use them for different things. I have a journal I write my adventures in, and another journal for thoughts and goals.
- Then I have the gratitude journal. Nothing is allowed in this journal except positive things I'm grateful for. I will write in it for 30 days straight, or sometimes even longer. I'll just simply write *today I am grateful*. Then I'll list a few things that happened to me for which I am grateful.

You see, I may not have that big mansion, but I have a house. Some people don't even have a house. If I had an apartment I would be grateful that I had an apartment, because some people don't have that. If you are reading this, then you are probably better off than you give yourself credit for.

My vehicle is reliable. I may not have a ranch of my own but do have a horse of my own, and that is pretty good right there. I may not be able to run a marathon, but my legs and my arms still work and I can hike 10 miles. I may not have a beach house in Hawaii, but I have been to Hawaii before, and had the opportunity to go with my entire family. That is incredible!

This works in every case for me. I am very fortunate. Looking back at every experience I can see that something good came of it.

Yes, I lost my grandparents, but at least I had such loving grandparents to lose. Many people don't get that opportunity. Those who don't get to know their own parents or grandparents have to deal with a whole other set of emotions.

If my truck had not been stolen, perhaps I wouldn't be driving the truck I love so much today. Maybe I was going to break down somewhere even worse in that truck later on. You see, I believe everything happens for a reason. I believe I was bullied and had so many painful dating experiences to help make me the person I am today.

Whenever a crisis happens in my family, we all grow closer together. We work harder to help each other, and become a stronger family. I can look at each and every experience now and turn a grateful eye towards it, instead of looking only at how bad it was. The more you work to realize this the more you will reprogram your thoughts and actions.

Every morning I wake up and tell myself that *today is going to be a good day!* Then I pray and meditate for all my loved ones, and ask that I can help positively influence the lives of all those I come in contact with. I ask to recognize opportunities to reach out to others in need, and to have the courage to act on those feelings. This may sound strange or odd, but I can promise you that karma will come back to you.

My mentor Marla Cilley, bestselling author and CEO of FlyLady.net told me, "When you continually give you will continually have." I used to always think this meant money, but now I know what it really means. It means happiness! When you reach out to others in need and give love and happiness, you will receive this back ten-fold.

Stop feeling sorry for yourself and start feeling grateful! It's really the key to happiness. It may take a few weeks to change your thoughts and maybe it will take months, *but you can change your thoughts*, and you will, if you want to. Gratitude is the key.

I want to include a few clips from my journal entries here. These were big things that happened, teaching me to shift my perception and be more grateful.

4-16-2013

Thank you, man at the ATM tonight, for teaching me a great lesson. I was in a hurry to get home to my warm house to eat dinner, driving my nice truck. You were taking your sweet time and I wanted you to hurry. Finally you peeled out of there in a humble rusty truck, and I thought to myself, *good—you got out of my way*. Then sadness overcame me as I saw the receipt in the ATM you left behind with the big words INSUFFICIENT FUNDS BALANCE $0.00. Many emotions came over me, but the main one was that I have it pretty good and shame on me for being irritated. I may not be rich but I can't complain. I certainly shouldn't be complaining that someone is taking his sweet time at an ATM. I remember when I used to live like that. I know how that feels. No matter what our problems are at the moment, the guy in front of us most likely has it much worse.

Thank you, man at the ATM. To this day I still have that receipt with the $0.00 balance on it, and it's where I'll always see it and remember.

9-11-2014

Today a desperate man died. You see, just this morning I was being down on myself for some financial situations where I was thinking I should have made much better choices! Don't get me wrong; I'm not doing badly but just wishing that things were better. Well, suddenly we started hearing reports of a bank robbery in progress. The suspect took some hostages and dumped his car in the subdivision where my house is, leaving the hostages, and running on foot. He had guns and was firing shots at officers. My nephews, who go to the schools nearby, were put on a full lockdown. At the elementary school all the kids were under their desks while the teachers covered the windows with papers. They brought in helicopters and began searching for this guy. They ended up finding him at the end of my street only a few houses down from where I live. There's a field where I walk my dog and he was hiding in the trees on the edge of the field. He began shooting at the police officers and so they had to protect themselves by shooting this man.

I am sitting here looking down my road and seeing all the investigators standing around this man. I can't help but wonder what he must have been going through; what he needed money for so bad for that he died for it. I feel very sad for him. Was he the victim of addiction, unemployment, or what? I feel so terrible for him even though he tormented an entire community today. There are no winners here.

I feel like we all have so much to be grateful for, and I tend to forget that. As I type this on my computer, sitting in my house, eating my pizza, I am feeling a whole lot more grateful for the decisions that I have made in my life.

2-14-15

This morning I woke up like every other day. Today was my Saturday Weight Watchers meeting that my mother puts on every week. I have my routine that I do every Saturday when I'm home. I wake up and tell myself to look for opportunities to help others in need this day. Then I take a dip in the hot tub before getting ready for the day, and head to the local gas station to get myself a giant diet soda and pick up a smaller diet soda for my sister.

Today was a bit different for me. As I was turning into the station there was a young man walking down the road towards it. He looked pretty normal, but I don't know why I noticed him really. It was nothing out of the ordinary. I went in, got my drinks and headed back to my truck.

As I got closer to my truck I saw that this same man was walking in the same direction. He said, "How are you? It's a very nice day, isn't it?"

I made my usual guarded small talk and continued to walk towards my truck, all the while wondering *why* he was talking to me. He kind of followed me and asked, "What direction are you headed."

I pointed and said *that way.*

He asked, "How far are you going?"

"Oh, not far," I answered. Now my guard was up and red flags were everywhere!

He then said, "Would you be willing to just drop me off anywhere along the way? Just as far as you drive? I'm headed that way and it would save me just that many more steps."

I have never in my life picked up a stranger or let anyone ride with me EVER. I would never even consider it. As I opened my mouth to tell him no, I was surprised to hear myself say *yes of course.* What was I thinking?

He was so happy and he shook my hand and said, "Thank you so much! My name is Kyle, what's yours?"

"Eric," I replied.

Unlocking my truck, I jumped in first. I didn't know whether to hold my phone or hide my papers that were in the truck or what. I was really out of my comfort zone here. I didn't know this guy at all.

He began to make small talk but I skirted around every question he asked me with very short and general answers. I just wanted this ride to be over. As I bounced the questions back to him I was amazed at how open and honest he was. How sincere and calm he was around me, who was also a stranger to him.

He then began to share his story. He said, "I am adopted. I came from California. I was very blessed to have a family adopt me and bring me to this good community."

He continued, "I have a past as I assume most of us do. I am not going to let my past ruin my future. I am not going to let it make me feel bad or hold me back. I want to live a better life. I have a 2-year-old son, and a twin sister who was also adopted, and I am blessed despite all I have been through. I just don't have the best of friends. Last night I was with some friends and it wasn't an ideal situation. They were all being stupid. Today they're all still sleeping it off. I asked if they were going to ever wake up and take me home, and they said they were just going to stay sleeping all day and I had to stay there. So I began to walk. I decided I needed to change my life and walk home. I can't live that way anymore. I need to slowly pull the thorns of my past out one at a time and realize how good God is for me, and realize how blessed I am. I need to change. I'm working on it."

He looked at me and said, "I can see that you are reading me. I see you too have thorns to pull out and you too are working to be a better person. I can see that you get me."

At this time we pulled up to my stop and he jumped out of the truck. He thanked me one more time, shook my hand, and away he went. He walked around the building and I never saw him again.

Kyle is an inspiration to me. I could see how much pain he held. I could tell he has had a very hard life and has been in situations that maybe I could never imagine. I could also see that he truly wants a better life for himself and I know that he is going to fight for it.

Thank you Kyle, for reminding me that we all hold our own thorns. It's time to pull them out and move on. The scars will last forever, but the thorns don't need to stay in. I have never and may never again take a stranger for a ride in my truck, but today I am grateful that I did.

20 SOLUTIONS

"F-E-A-R has two meanings:
Forget Everything And Run
or
Face Everything And Rise.
The choice is yours."
–Zig Ziglar

You have covered a whole lot of information in this book. As you have noticed, this is not a step-by-step recovery-style book. There is not a simple fix for the types of challenges we face. Everyone, including you, has their own set of challenges and own set of solutions. I can't just tell you to do this or do that, and then you will be there. It takes some effort from you.

There are so many things that I hope you get out of this book. Here is a list of things I used that have helped me so much in the past and continue to help me today. This will just be me listing many solutions that I hope that you will try. The most important thing is keeping up on your mental and physical health, as this has been instrumental to me. Eating right, exercising, being surrounded by like-minded healthy thinking people. This includes your family, friends, and associations.

If you are constantly surrounded by negative people you will also be negative. It's said by many of my mentors that you will become the average of the top 5 people you spend the most time with. If this is true, I strongly suggest you look at your associations, and quickly. Reading positive books and listening to positive audio messages as I drive around have been huge for me. I learned these principles from Darren Hardy—author, speaker, and publisher of *Success Magazine*.

I stopped watching the news and listening to depressing sad music, at least most of the time. I hike, started doing different types of yoga, began walking my dog, started swimming laps in a local pool. I tried new things and became more impulsive. You really should try changing up your routine. Do it for just one day. It will be so liberating for you.

Do nice things for other people. This is HUGE and will change your life. Pray often or meditate if you don't pray, or do both. Take daily time-outs for slow controlled breathing.

Free your mind of stress and yes, talk to yourself. Say positive things to yourself and tell yourself *it's going to be a great day.*

Get lots of sleep. This was one of the most important for me. You need to decide on a time and go to bed on a regular schedule. Try to get at least 7 or 8 hours of sleep every night.

Take your vitamins. Sometimes vitamin deficiencies can cause you to have anxiety and depression problems. This helped me out so much.

Make sure you are always writing in your journal. We have talked about how important journals can be. Don't think you have to create a work of art; this is for you.

Be sure to set goals for yourself. Pick out a few goals and go for them. When you have goals you are looking forward instead of backward.

Find some things you like to do. I started to ride my bike, go camping more, smile at strangers, change my routine, and do all the above activities. This changed my life dramatically and it will change yours too. Just try some of these things.

Keep your own list of solutions, and add things to it as you experiment and learn.

21 CONCLUSION: THE POINT

"Inaction breeds doubt and fear. Action breeds confidence
and courage. If you want to conquer fear, do not sit home
and think about it. Go out and get busy."
—Dale Carnegie

Why did I tell you all these stories? What was the point of this whole book? What did you get out of it?

In all reality, as I was writing this book I told myself that it needed to be written. It needed to be written for all of those who suffer from and deal with fear, depression, and anxiety. If even one person gets anything out of it and improves their life, then this entire labor of love was well worth it.

It's been said that life begins on the other side of fear. This is something that has been proven true for myself over and over again. By facing my fears one day at a time my life began to transform into the life that I always dreamed about.

As I wrote, I was able to see how each of these experiences or periods of time in my life created the walls that held me back from living the life of my dreams. I can pin each of my fears to those experiences— my fear of loss, fear of love, fear of acceptance, and many other fears— and I have gone from a kid who believed he could do anything, to becoming an overweight and hopelessly depressed adult, and then back to a grown-up who believes he can do anything! I have achieved many of my dreams and far exceeded some of them. My depression has been well-managed over the past several years, and I'm not done in my pursuit, either.

Life is hard. It always will be hard. There's so much good mixed in with the bad. I wouldn't trade my past or my experiences for anything, and I know that you have just as many incredible stories as I do.

We have two choices—fight for happiness, or give up. I choose to fight for happiness and my hope is that you do as well. Yet there were many times I thought about giving up. I remind myself each day that I need to always fight. And I always ask myself questions. Yes, sometimes out loud. You might think that all I do is talk to myself. Well, I do, kind of! I ask myself things such as, *why not see what I can do?* Why not see if I can change my circumstances? Why not change my routine, or change my attitude? Why not just give something else a try and start to make a change? Why not now? Why not today? Today is the day—right now is the time! There's no better time than *right this very second* to decide what you want to do with your life. And maybe you do want to do something better.

That's how I lost 80 pounds. That's how I got up the nerve to stand on a stage and sing. And that's how I got over my fear of speaking. I have faced so many of my fears. I have rappelled on a mountainside, rode crazy bucking horses, rode my horse into the backwoods and slept under the pine trees on the ground. I've experienced so much life, and that's what living is about. Life truly is for the living.

What will it take to make you happy? Maybe it's something you want to do less of. Maybe it's something you want to do more of. What will you regret not doing at the end of your life? Let's face it—we do all have regrets, but if you are reading this book, there is still time. It's just a matter of making a decision.

You see, many times I was faced with making tough decisions; we all are. And many times I was on the fence about something. I'm still on the fence with some decisions and may always be. That's life right there! Not a day goes by without old demons from the past that try to come bubbling back up. I have to fight depression and anxiety from time to time, but now I have the tools to do so.

Have I won the war? No; I'm still fighting and will always be fighting. Even when I feel like I have won or have the upper hand it's important to keep fighting! Do I feel I can move ahead and continue to create the life of my dreams? *Absolutely!* I feel this way because I've done it multiple times, and so have you. I know that you have just as many stories and most likely, even more hardships than I could possibly imagine. If I heard your story, I would be so amazingly inspired. There are millions of people, actually more like billions of people, who have had it so much worse. There are more people than you can count who have risen above hardships and trials that many of us could not even wrap our minds around. They are my heroes and they inspire me every day. You inspire me too! By writing this book and sharing my stories, I simply hope that I'm able to help even one person ask these questions:

How can I break free? How can I make sure I don't miss the good stuff? Why not me? Why not today?

You can do it. I have no doubt about that. The only thing holding you back is you. Why not today? Today is your day.

"All our dreams can come true if we
have the courage to pursue them."
—Walt Disney

One of my first Anti-Bully assemblies.

My Band.

ABOUT THE AUTHOR

Eric Dodge's albums are making waves in the country music world! His album Why Not Today became an international success and has sold worldwide in over 15 countries, even topping the Amazon.com Best Selling Albums list. Eric has also been featured in *Country Weekly* magazine, KUTV 2 News at Noon, and Good Things Utah.

Eric has released 8 albums and has performed across the United States and Canada. In 2012 he was accepted into the Country Music Association (CMA). In 2013 Eric became an author and entered the world of writing, releasing his debut book titled *Baby Steps To Music Industry Success.*

Eric is also a member of the National Speakers Association (NSA), sharing his musical messages in Keynote and Corporate events all across the United States. He's also shared the stage with many of country music's biggest names, including Clint Black, Lorrie Morgan, Pam Tillis, SHeDAISY, Julianne Hough, John Michael Montgomery, Justin Moore, Collin Raye, Chris LeDoux, Diamond Rio, Terri Clark, Travis Tritt, and Carrie Underwood.

www.EricDodge.com

Follow us everywhere at ericdodge.com.

For more information on Eric Dodge or to order bulk copies of his books, CDs, or download his music, go to ericdodge.com.

To contact Eric Dodge about concert requests, speaking engagements, or media requests please visit ericdodge.com.

435-674-4319

management@ericdodge.com

Made in the USA
San Bernardino, CA
16 September 2015